How To Eliminate Achievement Gap Without Leaving Any Child Behind

STUDENT EDITION: A HANDBOOK OF STRATEGIES AND BEST PRACTICES

Ignatius E. Idio, Ph.D.

Bloomington, IN  Milton Keynes, UK

authorHOUSE®

AuthorHouse™
1663 Liberty Drive, Suite 200
Bloomington, IN 47403
www.authorhouse.com
Phone: 1-800-839-8640

AuthorHouse™ *UK Ltd.*
500 Avebury Boulevard
Central Milton Keynes, MK9 2BE
www.authorhouse.co.uk
Phone: 08001974150

First published by AuthorHouse 4/12/2007

ISBN: 978-1-4259-9573-7 (sc)

Library of Congress Control Number: 2007901365

Printed in the United States of America
Bloomington, Indiana

This book is printed on acid-free paper.

CONTENTS

PART TWO

CONTENT OVERVIEW

Part One.   *How to Eliminate Achievement Gap Without Leaving Any Child Behind: A Handbook of Strategies and Best Practices* is organized into two parts. Part one contains five chapters. The chapters are compatible, giving the teacher the flexibility to adapt the concepts to a variety of instructional progression. Part two contains ancillary materials such as the black line masters for both teachers and students use. Part two also has test banks and answer keys to be included in the teacher's edition.

Chapter 1.   **Instructional Strategies** presents eleven proven, research-based, and practical strategies for teachers to adapt to their teaching to ensure that all students experience academic success by enabling each student to acquire and present knowledge in a differentiated classroom. Chapter 1 begins with *smart goal* and the components of effective lesson plan to specific strategies that teachers and students can use to enhance teaching and learning in the classroom.

Chapter 2.   **Assessment of Classroom Learning** stresses the fact that more testing rather than less testing has become the norm instead of the exception. Chapter 2 addresses contemporary issues such as: *Why should teachers assess student learning? Do students really learn the specific curricular objectives that teachers are teaching? How do teachers and instructors know whether or not students are really learning and mastering the concepts that they are teaching?* In addition to addressing the issues that relate to classroom assessment, this chapter presents the different assessment tools that are readily available to teachers to use in assessing classroom learning.

Chapter 3.   **Classroom Management** describes several strategies that research has shown to be effective in maintaining discipline, actively engaging students in the learning process, and managing student and teacher behaviors in order to achieve instructional goal and objectives at the end of each school day. Chapter 3 also identifies effective classroom procedures and routines, specific incidents that are related to classroom management, triggers of student misbehavior, and purpose or function of misbehavior in the classroom. It describes what teachers can do to bring student back to equilibrium if and when a student misbehaves or distracts in the classroom. Chapter 3 discusses effective rewards and consequences that have proven to promote time on task and support learning. It describes different ways through which teachers communicate consistently with parents. The last part of chapter three contains four group activities in which veteran teachers, interns, and teacher education majors can work on to hone their classroom management skills.

Chapter 4. What Some States, School Districts, and Schools are Doing to Narrow **Achievement Gap** provides evidence of the different things that states, local districts, and individual schools are doing to narrow the achievement gaps. Chapter 4 identifies Missouri, North Carolina, Texas, Indiana, and Nevada, Georgia as examples of states that are making great strides in closing the achievement gaps between the minority students and their white counterparts. Chapter 4 further identifies the individual schools that are taking great steps in narrowing the achievement gaps in our schools. Examples of identified schools include the Department of defense (DoD) schools, El Paso, Texas schools, and Lanier Middle School in Houston.

Chapter 5. **A Summary of Research Findings about What Works in Teaching and Learning** summarizes the research findings that suggest what works well with teaching and learning. Several of these research findings have been implemented by teachers in our schools to improve academic achievement for all students.

Part Two. **Ancillary Materials/Teaching and Learning Tools with Duplicable Back Line Masters** are included for teachers and students to use as needed to enhance teaching and learning in the classroom in order to reach the ultimate goal of academic achievement for all students without leaving any child behind. The test banks and answer keys are included in part two for the teacher's edition.

FORWARD

The purpose of schooling is to develop and enrich children's and adult's knowledge, skills, values, and attitude in order for them to grow and contribute to life in a democratic society. *How to Eliminate Achievement Gap Without Leaving Any Child Behind: A Handbook of Strategies and Best Practices* will provide you with an understanding of instruction from a variety of expert perspectives. It will also benefit experienced teachers to become the best in their profession. This edition will bring you the latest innovations and insights concerning the best instructional practices.

This book is appropriate for traditional and nontraditional students who are transitioning to a second career, either in the context of undergraduate program or of a post baccalaureate program. The author sees teachers as a valuable source of information and ideas that should be shared with all current and prospective teaching professionals. I trust that you will find this book applicable to both your current and future teaching and learning endeavors.

The text is organized to progress from a focus on the innovative teaching and instructional strategies, skills and constructivist teaching in Chapter 1. Chapter 2 focuses on assessment practices and types of assessment. Chapter 3 reviews types of behavior that disrupt teaching and prevent learning. The nature of "misbehavior" and its effects on students and teachers are discussed. Practical solutions to solve misbehavior problems are also suggested. Chapter 4 focuses on what the state and federal government are doing to close the achievement gap between the minority, disadvantaged students and their majority, more affluent counterparts. Chapter 5 shares conclusions from the research findings about what works in teaching and learning. I hope that the practices suggested in this book will be helpful to you and your student.

Dr. Joseph P. Akpan
Mount Vernon Nazarene University
Mount Vernon, Ohio.

PREFACE

Since the mid-1980s, state and federal government policymakers have made school reform a top priority. This effort has made important gains, but significant challenges still lay ahead. For instance, the "achievement gap" is one such challenge that continues to haunt our schools. The preceding scenario inspired the author to write *How to Eliminate Achievement Gap Without Leaving Any Child Behind: A Handbook of Strategies and Best Practices.*

What is the achievement gap?

For our purpose, the achievement gap is defined as the persistent disparity in academic achievement between the minority and disadvantaged students and the students of Caucasian (white) and Asian descents. For example, in the U.S. the children from economically disadvantaged households are, for the most part, at the bottom of achievement scale.

Historical perspective

As a minority group, African-American students have come a long way and have overcome a plethora of racial barriers to get to where they are today. In 1896, the U.S. Supreme Court ruled that to have "separate but equal" schools for black and white students was legal. By then, schools for African Americans were often poor and rundown (Dr. Berkin C. et al., 2003).

In 1954, the U.S. Supreme Court reversed itself in the ***Brown v. Board of Education*** decision that **"separate but equal"** was unconstitutional. The Apex Court's ruling sparked negative reactions among white politicians. For instance, in Virginia, a powerful Senator and a former Governor of the Commonwealth of Virginia, Harry F. Byrd, Sr., disagreed with the ruling and led the massive resistance movement against school integration.

In 1950s, several schools in Virginia were shut down rather than integrate. Prince Edward County had no public schools from 1959 through 1963. To enforce the 1954 Supreme Court's *Brown v. Board* of Education decision in support of desegregation and integration of schools, the U.S. marshals escorted African American students to white only schools.

New exigency at the federal stage

Recently, the federal government has weighed in on the fray. "Recent changes in Federal education policy have put achievement gap on the national spotlights. The **No**

Child Left Behind Act (NCLB) requires states to set the same performance standard for all children" (NCLB, 2002) and to close the achievement gap. The NCLB sets the same performance target for children "from economically disadvantaged families, with learning disabilities, with limited English proficiency, and from all major ethnic and racial groups."

Consequences for not meeting Targets

"Within a school, if any student subgroup persistently fails to meet performance targets, districts must provide public school choice and supplemental services to those students and eventually restructure the school's governance. That is required even if the school performs well overall. Schools now are considered successful only if they close the achievement gap" (NCLB, 2002).

The achievement gap between minority students and their white peers is evident in standardized test score data as reported by several school districts, the National Assessment for Education Progress (NAEP), and the National Center for Educational Statistics (NCES).

Overarching question and purpose of this book

The overarching question this book will attempt to answer is: Can schools ever close or eliminate the achievement gap between minority students such as African Americans, Latinos, and their white Caucasians and Asian American counterparts? Or, "Can schools narrow the black-white test score gap?" (Ferguson, R. F., 1998). Therefore, the purpose of this book includes the following aims:

- To procure promising research-based best instructional practices and make them available to teachers and schools for use in teaching all students to meet and exceed the standards set by the "No Child Left Behind (NCLB Act, 2002)
- To share with colleague educators, particularly the first year teachers successful instructional practices, strategies, and professional experiences acquired by this author (a veteran teacher of K-12 schools and college) from years of implementation of the school curriculums and participation in professional development programs
- To highlight the accountability systems initiated by several state departments of education and school districts in order to hold schools responsible for educating all students based on high standards and to continuously improve academic performance with intent to ultimately eliminate achievement gap between various student subgroups. Finally, the author has some encouraging words for the college instructor, for the teacher education students and interns, and for the classroom teacher

To The College Instructor

This text is designed primarily for a one-semester course on instructional and classroom management strategies using research-based and best instructional practice resources. It provides more ready-to-use materials for the instructor to use in preparing the college of education majors and teacher interns for the actual classroom teaching experience. The book can be used as a companion text for a method course in teaching.

The instructor may progress through the text in sequence from Chapter 1: Instructional Strategies, Chapter 2: Assessment of Classroom Learning, Chapter 3: Classroom Management, Chapter 4: What States Are doing to Narrow the Achievement Gap, and Chapter 5: A Summary of Research Findings about What Works in Teaching and Learning. Since the chapters and concepts are compatible, the instructor may choose to teach any of the chapters in no particular order. Irrespective of the sequence followed in teaching the contents of this book, the instructor needs to cover all of the concepts in each chapter.

The Teacher's Edition contains test banks, corresponding answer keys, and ancillary resources including black line masters of charts and maps which are readily available for the instructor's use to teach the course without reinventing additional materials. The student's edition does not include the test bank and corresponding answer keys.

To The Teacher Education Students and Interns

As you prepare to assume the most challenging calling of your professional career, you need to be well prepared. Teaching is constantly evolving, and you are an agent of change in our global society. Teachers are expected to be highly trained, knowledgeable about the curriculum and instruction, assessment of classroom learning, and classroom management. Today there is a lot at stake in teaching our youngsters to prepare them to become leaders and productive citizens of our nation. You will be held accountable for student success and responsible for closing the achievement gap among student groups and subgroups within the school system. Throughout your teaching, you will be accountable to the following stakeholders, namely your building supervisors, school district, state, the federal governments, parents and the tax payers. In order to perform well on your teaching profession, you should learn very extensively about teaching and learning while you are in college so that you will be confident when you first step foot into the classroom full of students you will be responsible for during the school year. To help you prepare for your teaching experience in the classroom, the author is sharing his years of classroom experience with you in this book: *How to Eliminate Achievement Gap Without Leaving Any Child Behind: A Handbook of Strategies and Best Practices.* This book contains practical, easy-to-use, and user-friendly black line masters you can utilize to enhance your learning. There are group activities that simulate real classroom behavior problems for you to practice with. You can also use the resources and suggestions in the book to help you during your student teaching (practicum) experience.

To The Classroom Teacher

You are there in the trenches with the children in your trust. You encounter on a daily basis with the good, the not so good, and the unexpected. If you have survived the first three years of your teaching experience, you have made it, and I commend you for your willingness to make a difference in the lives of our children. You and the rest of the veteran teachers have a lot in common. Like most professionals, you know when your work day starts. That is where the similarity ends. Believe it or not, teachers' work days do not end at eight o'clock P.M. It ends when you have expended all of the energy cleaning and arranging rooms, planning the next day's lessons, checking papers, calling or returning parents' telephone calls, answering e-mail messages, filing office papers, attending meetings and workshops, sponsoring extramural activities, and then oops! Then you realize that there are still tests and quizzes to be created or checked, weekly progress reports to be done, midterm and final grades to be recorded, quarterly and final report cards to be done. In order to meet deadlines, you must take unfinished work home to continue to work late at night to get it ready for school the next day. Figure in family responsibility – attending to your family needs. Does this scenario sound familiar?

To make your instructional day more fulfilling and manageable, *How to Eliminate Achievement Gap Without Leaving Any Child Behind: A Handbook of Strategies and Best Practices was written with you in mind.* In the book, you will find research-based, ready-to-use, and proven instructional tools you can use with your students throughout the year. The author of this book has used these instructional materials with students and has witnessed increased academic achievement for all students. Since using the ideas and instructional tools contained in this book, the achievement gap between students in his class has practically been eliminated. He feels comfortable to confide in you that some of the instructional ideas suggested in this book have been collected from the following sources - seminars, workshops, observation of and collaboration with other colleague teachers - during his teaching years in K-12 setting and as a college instructor. If you are a presenter at staff development activities, the group activities, the test banks, and corresponding answer keys contained in part two of the book are available for you to use.

Feel free to copy the black line masters as they relate to instructional strategies, assessment of classroom learning, and classroom management for use with your students as you strive daily to close the achievement gap among students and student subgroups in your classroom. Finally, use the comment/suggestion form in the back of the book to inform us about your experience after you have taught the contents of the book. Your comments will be integrated into the next edition of this book.

Dr. Ignatius E. Idio
Prince William Public Schools &Northern Virginia Community College,
Manassas, Virginia

ACKNOWLEDGMENTS

I wish to acknowledge the contributions of my colleagues who have provided encouragement, advice, and suggestions for this edition of *How to Eliminate Achievement Gap Without Leaving Any Child Behind: A Handbook of Strategies and Best Practices*: Joyce Boyd (Principal), Rachel Perry and Dawn Johnson, Pennington Traditional School, Manassas, Virginia; Dr. Joseph P. Akpan, Mount Vernon Nazarene University, Ohio. Dr. Akpan wrote the forward to this book.

I am particularly indebted to the fourth graders in Room 5 with whom I tested the validity and success of the strategies and best practices suggested in this book and specifically, to those students who granted their permission for me to include their reflective writings in this book: Audrey Lyle, Chelsea Gana, Michael Manley, and Rebecca Ennis, Pennington Traditional School, Manassas, Virginia.

A special thanks goes to Adele Brinkley, Sunny Side, Georgia for her impeccable attention to details while editing the text to ensure that all visible errors were corrected. Finally, I take full responsibility for any mistakes that might have been unintentionally omitted.

DEDICATION

This book is dedicated to Ignatius, Francisca, Victoria, Stephanie, and Edemekong Esema-Idio and to past, present, and future educators for their encouragement and services to our children and our nation.

PART ONE

"The man (person) who can make hard things happen is the educator."

~Ralph Waldo Emerson

CHAPTER 1
Instructional Strategies

This chapter describes the instructional practices that several teachers including the author of this book, have used in their classrooms to ensure that all students attain academic achievement at the end of instruction, regardless of the racial makeup, economic situations, and home environments of the students. Chapter 1 further describes what many school districts are currently doing to narrow the achievement gap, with ultimate goal to eliminate the minority-white test score gap as mandated by the federal government education policy, in the No Child Left Behind Act of 2002.

From _S.M.A.R.T_ Goal to Effective Lesson Plan

_S.M. A.R.T_ is an acronym for the following conceptual key words that constitute a goal statement (see teaching and learning tools page for sample goal statements). It includes the following:

Specific Strategies – State the specific curriculum materials and resources available for use in instructional activities

Measurable – States in measurable quantity, such as the percentage of knowledge acquisition by the learners after the lesson is taught

Attainable – States the focus of the lesson

Results – State that the strategies used to implement the lesson are _consistent_ and _reliable_ in order to give similar results at the end of instruction

Time Bound – States the time frame for achieving the goal of the instruction

Effective Lesson Plan

An effective lesson plan should address the why, what, how, and when questions. A good lesson plan should ask

- Why should the lesson be taught?
- What prior knowledge and experience do students have about the concepts of the lesson?
- What should students learn and be able to learn at the end of the lesson?
- How will teachers determine if students really learn the concept?
- How will students demonstrate what they learn and what to do with the knowledge?
- When will teachers assess student mastery of the curriculum concepts?
- When will teachers differentiate instruction to ensure that all students learn the concept?
- When is the appropriate time to introduce a new knowledge, concepts, and skills?

The Components of a Lesson Plan

- Lesson title
- Purpose
- Anticipatory set – Access prior knowledge, set the stage
- Materials – Curriculum materials/resources relevant to instruction
- Goal (see *S.M.A.R.T.* goal)
- Objectives – Specific achievable skills students will learn
- Essential questions – Questions around which lesson concepts revolve
- Essential Attributes/knowledge – What the students will acquire
- Essential skills – Specific skills that students will master
- Independent Practice – Students engage in activities to demonstrate learning
- Assessment/Evaluation --
    1. Formative (quiz, chapter test, observation, check list, question/answer)
    2. Summative (State standardized tests, criteria referenced tests, norm-referenced tests, curriculum management system or CMS tests
- Closure – Summary of important concepts taught and learned and connection to new ideas
- Home work as necessary for further practice of skills to reinforce learning

Summarizing Strategies That Work

> *"I can't understand why people are frightened*
> *of new ideas; I'm frightened by the old ones."*
> *~ John Cage*

STRATEGY #1

THE 3 - 2 - 1 STRATEGY

The 3-2-1 strategy (Rutherford, P., 2002), is used to teach students how to summarize important points in a learning process.

The teacher or instructor may provide opportunities for students to write or illustrate the following as evidence of learning and understanding the concepts taught. Write or state:

3   most important events in the story

2   questions you would like to ask the character in the story

1   event in this book that reminds you of another book you have read

Each stem of the 3-2-1- strategy can be designed to correspond to the level of thinking at which the teacher expects learner to be.

Source: Adapted from Paula Rutherford, ©*Just ASK Publication,* ASK Inc, 2002.

"Learning is a treasure that will follow its owner everywhere."
— *Chinese Proverb*

STRATEGY #2

THINKING STRATEGY THAT WORKS
QUESTION – THINK – PAIR – SHARE   STRATEGY

The think-pair-share strategy works like this.

Question
The teacher asks a question.

Think
Students have 30 to 60 seconds to think about possible answers to the question.

Pair
Students pair up with a neighbor to discuss their thinking in 2 to 3 minutes. They may write their discussion down on paper.

Share
The teacher asks students to share their responses with the whole class or within a small group of students for about 2 to 5 minutes.

Advantages to the teacher
- Allows teachers to check for understanding
- Provides time to adjust instruction
- Creates time to locate resources to support instruction
- Allows time to interact with one or two students while the rest of the class work
- Allows opportunities to evaluate students' levels of thinking

Advantages to students
- Provides time for students to process the information
- Builds in wait time
- Allows time to rehearse the discussion
- Encourages depth and breadth of thought
- Provides a non-intimidating setting for student participation
- Builds self-esteem in students

Source: Adapted from Paula Rutherford, ©*Just ASK Publication,* ASK Inc, 2002.

> *"Only the educated are free."*
> *(Epictetus* A.D. 50?-138?),
> a Greek Stoic philosopher

STRATEGY #3

USING GRAPHIC ORGANIZERS TO REPRESENT KNOWLEDGE

According to psychologists and learning theorists, we store knowledge in two ways: linguistically and non-linguistically (Marzano, 2001). That is, we store what we know in ways associated with words (the linguistic form and with images or graphics (the non-linguistic form). Students can learn to use graphics to represent knowledge.

After modeling the process for students, teachers can teach students how to use graphics or idea charts to describe specific concepts such as people, places, events, things, and ideas. The charts below describe the famous people.

President Thomas Jefferson

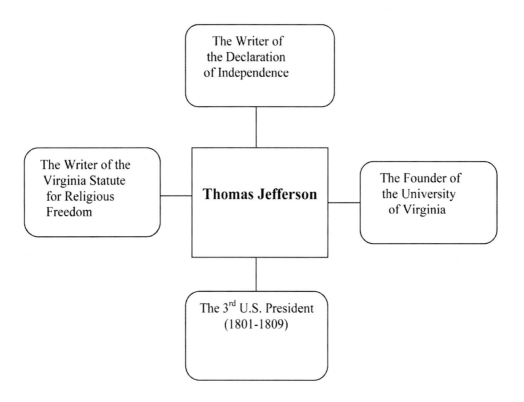

STRATEGY #4

MR. NELSON MANDELA

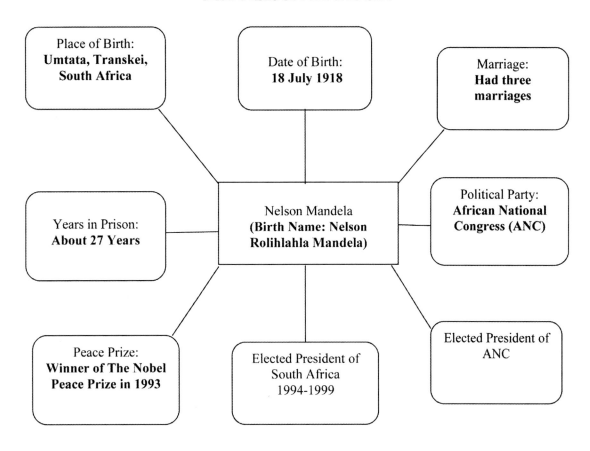

STRATEGY #5

MADAM PRESIDENT
OF LIBERIA, WEST AFRICA

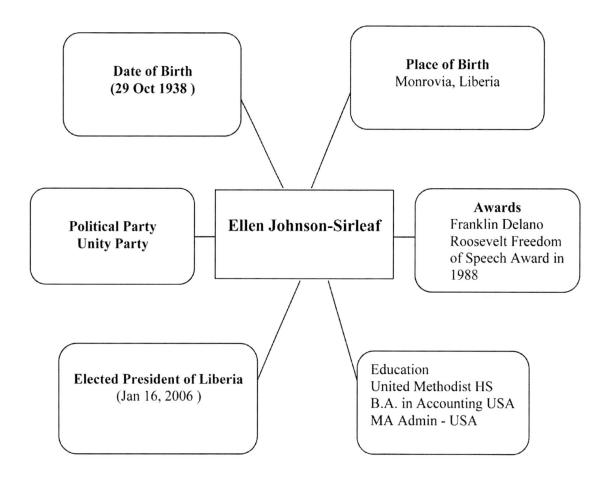

Date of Birth
(29 Oct 1938)

Place of Birth
Monrovia, Liberia

Political Party
Unity Party

Ellen Johnson-Sirleaf

Awards
Franklin Delano
Roosevelt Freedom
of Speech Award in
1988

Elected President of Liberia
(Jan 16, 2006)

Education
United Methodist HS
B.A. in Accounting USA
MA Admin - USA

> *"When we level the instructional playing field, all learners can successfully perform at their vantage points."*
> *~ Dr. Ignatius E. Idio, 2006*

STRATEGY #6

Writing Process In Sequence

The steps in the writing process include the following: *getting started, planning, drafting, revising, editing, proofreading, and submitting.* Writing never follows a linear path. Do not expect to travel smoothly through the steps in the writing process. Therefore, writing involves "detours, wrong turns, and repeated visits" (Vandermey, R. et. al., 2004). This chart describes the steps in the writing process. These steps often overlap in the flowchart. During writing, you will sometimes travel back and forth within steps.

SEQUENCE CHART

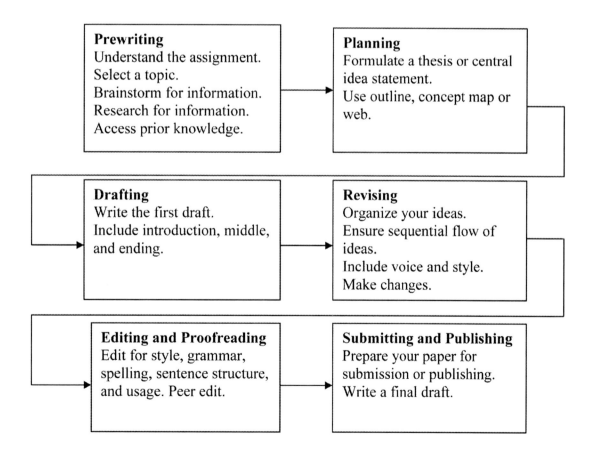

Prewriting
Understand the assignment.
Select a topic.
Brainstorm for information.
Research for information.
Access prior knowledge.

Planning
Formulate a thesis or central idea statement.
Use outline, concept map or web.

Drafting
Write the first draft.
Include introduction, middle, and ending.

Revising
Organize your ideas.
Ensure sequential flow of ideas.
Include voice and style.
Make changes.

Editing and Proofreading
Edit for style, grammar, spelling, sentence structure, and usage. Peer edit.

Submitting and Publishing
Prepare your paper for submission or publishing.
Write a final draft.

"Critical thinking rejuvenates the brain."
- Dr. Ignatius E. Idio, 2006

STRATEGY #7

Brainstorming For Writing Ideas Using A Brainstorming Chart

A brainstorming chart is used to brainstorm ideas and for accessing prior knowledge about a topic. It can be used to help define a thing or idea.

BRAINSTORMING CHART

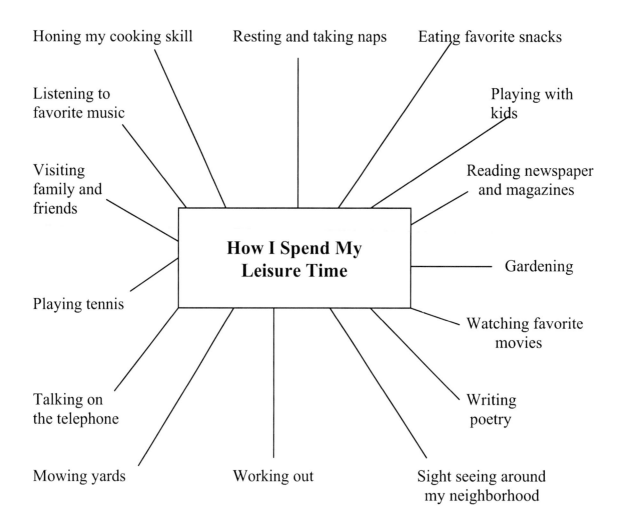

STRATEGY #8

Using Bloom's Taxonomy To Ask Higher Order Level Questions

Often times, teachers ask students questions in the "knowledge" level of Bloom's Taxonomy almost "80% to 90% of the time" (Bloom, et al., 1956). The purpose of this section is to explore the higher-level questions and to encourage teachers to use the following six-question categories as defined by Howard Bloom, a learning theorist and psychologist.

BLOOM'S TAXANOMY

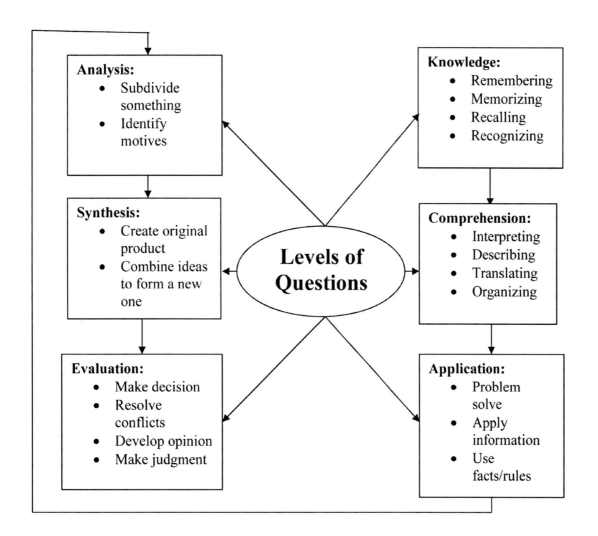

SAMPLE QUESTIONS

In order to motivate all students to think critically, teachers need to vary the level of questioning by "compacting" (modifying) the curriculum to accommodate differences in ability and readiness. "Compacting the curriculum means modifying the contents of the curriculum. It sometimes requires assessing a student's knowledge, skills, attitudes, and providing alternative activities for the student who has already mastered the curriculum contents. This can be achieved by pre-testing basic concepts or using performance assessment test methods" (Theroux, P., 2004). A quick and easy way to vary the level of questioning is to put six posters on the classroom walls with the Bloom's Taxonomy of Higher Order Level Questions as listed below. These posters will be useful cues for teachers to refer students to during class discussion, research questions, depending on student's ability or assignment requirements.

KNOWLEDGE
- Who is the main character in the story?
- What is the setting for the story?

COMPREHENSION
- What is the meaning of the phrase "To be or not to be?"
- Can you restate the main idea in your own word?

APPLICATION
- Why is it important to be able to use figure of speech such as simile and metaphor in writing?
- Can you create a fun game or activity for a kindergarten teacher to use with her students?

ANALYSIS
- What are the parts of an insect?
- Can you classify these words according to their parts of speech?
- How are fiction and nonfiction texts alike and different? (Compare-Contrast)

SYNTHESIS
- What can you infer from the statement: "Give me liberty or give me death" by Patrick Henry?
- Can you predict or hypothesize which is heavier, oil or water?
- What will happen if oil and water are mixed together?

EVALUATION
- Do you agree or disagree with the illegal or non-documented immigrants for protesting the government in April 2006 to grant them amnesty or citizenship?
- Can you arrange the following objects in order of priority?
- What do you think about Iranians acquiring nuclear weapons? (Adapted from Broom, et al., 1956).

When and Why Teachers Should Ask Questions

The reason we ask questions is to probe for understanding and determine comprehension of the concept, theme, or information that is taught.

Use questions prior to learning experiences:

- To initiate a discussion
- To stimulate student curiosity
- To focus students on a new concept or a different aspect of a concept
- To access prior knowledge and experience
- To consolidate previous learning
- To clarify misconceptions
- To teach students the skill of questioning

Use questions during and after learning experiences:

- To break down complex tasks and issues
- To promote transfer and retention
- To control shifts in discussions
- To keep discussions on track
- To invite student questions
- To elicit student opinions
- To promote interaction
- To facilitate flexible thinking
- To challenge the obvious
- To check for understanding
- To help students confront their misconceptions and reframe their thinking
- To focus on process
- To promote student evaluation of credibility of sources and validity of evidence
- To cause students to consider alternative perspectives

- To help students make connections
- To develop critical thinking skill in students
- To facilitate the learning process

Source: Adapted from Paula Rutherford, ©*Just ASK Publication,* ASK Inc, 2002

Samples of Important and Purposeful Questions

- Based on what you know about this topic, what can you predict about the story?
- Why is this one more important than that one?
- How does this one compare with that one?
- What else can you infer from the story?
- How are they different and alike?
- How can you find out?
- Why do you think this one is better than the other one?
- What if you …?
- Can you tell more?
- How did you arrive at that conclusion?
- How would you feel if …?
- Suppose … then what?
- Does what you discover make you think differently and why?
- What do you need to do next?
- Does this story or book remind you of another story or book you have read?
- When have you done or experienced something similar to this one?
- What do you think causes …?
- Certainly, you are correct, but how did you know that it was right?
- What do you think the problem is?
- Can you think of another way that you can do this?
- What do you think is the central idea or theme of this story?
- For what do you think you can use the information?
- How can you use this information?
- Do you think the same procedure can be used to solve algebraic problems?

Source: Adapted from Paula Rutherford, ©*Just ASK Publication,* ASK Inc, 2002

> *"No two children are alike. No two children learn in the identical way. An enriched environment for one student is not necessarily enriched for another.*
> *~ Marian Diamond, 1998*

STRATEGY #9

DIFFERENTIATED INSTRUCTION STRATEGY

Differentiated instruction here is "creating multiple paths to ensure that all students with diverse abilities , interest, or learning needs experience equally appropriate ways to absorb, use, develop, and present concepts as a part of the daily learning process" (Theroux, P., 2004). A teacher who differentiates instruction will structure his or her classroom environment to encourage all students to assume greater responsibility and ownership for their own learning. A differentiated classroom provides opportunities for collaborative or peer teaching and cooperative learning.

Ways to Differentiate Instruction

A teacher can differentiate instruction in the content or topic, process, product, and classroom environment *(Marian Diamond, 1998).*

1. Differentiation by Content/Topic

```
                              ┌──────────────────────┐
                              │ Teachers compact the │
                              │ curriculum or pretest│
              ┌────────────┐  │ students to identify │
              │ Knowledge  │→ │ those who do not need│
              │ we want    │  │ direct instruction.  │
              │ students to│  └──────────────────────┘
              │ acquire    │  ┌──────────────────────┐
              └────────────┘  │ Teachers assess      │
           ↗                → │ students' prior      │
   ┌──────────────┐           │ knowledge of the     │
   │ CONTENT/TOPIC│           │ concept.             │
   └──────────────┘           └──────────────────────┘
           ↘                  ┌──────────────────────┐
              ┌────────────┐  │ Students who         │
              │ Skills we  │→ │ demonstrate          │
              │ want       │  │ understanding of the │
              │ students to│  │ concept can skip the │
              │ learn      │  │ instruction step and │
              └────────────┘  │ move to apply the    │
                              │ concept to a given   │
                              │ task.                │
                              └──────────────────────┘
                              ┌──────────────────────┐
                              │ The apt students are │
                              │ permitted to         │
                            → │ accelerate           │
                              │ independently on some│
                              │ project in order to  │
                              │ cover the content    │
                              │ faster than their    │
                              │ peers.               │
                              └──────────────────────┘
```

2. Differentiation by Process/Activities

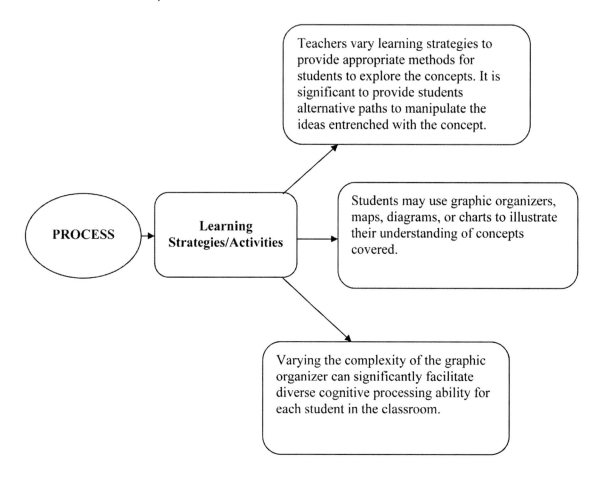

3. Differentiation by the Product

Performance Expectation

Differentiating by the product means varying the complexity of the product that students create in order to demonstrate mastery of the concepts (See: http://www.rogertaylor.com/reference/Product-Grid.pdf).

PRODUCT

Offer Students Option or Choice
Teachers assign products that require greater levels of independence. Students who are working below grade level may have reduced performance expectations. Those who are above grade level can be expected to produce work that requires more advanced thinking.

Motivation
Teachers offer assignments that are more open-ended in nature. Sometimes, it is motivating to offer students choice of products or final outputs and yet meet the requirements for learning the concepts.

4. Differentiation by Manipulating the Environment or Accommodating Individual Learning Style

Learning styles can be classified as *"sensory, perceptual, cognitive information processing, personality, personal talents, and situational"* (Theroux, P., 2004).

- Sensory - Based on Dunn and Dunn's Learning Styles Inventory, sensory learning style focuses on identifying relevant stimuli that influence learning and by changing the learning environment to suit the students learning styles.
- Perceptual - Students are either left or right brain dominant. That is, some students learn more using their right brain as opposed to left brain.
- Cognitive Information Processing - Students process information by sensing//intuitive; visual/verbal; active/reflective; and sequential/global methods (Kolb's Model).
- Personality – Meyers-Briggs Type Indicator and Kersley's Temperament Sorter focused on how people's personality impact how they interact with others in a learning environment.
- Personal Talents – Based on Howard Gardner's (1994) Multiple Intelligences, some students learn best using linguistic, logical-mathematic, spatial, bodily-kinesthetic, musical, interpersonal, intrapersonal, and naturalist intelligences.
- Situational – Regardless of a person's natural learning styles or talents, it is significant to be cognizant of the fact that some tasks demand specialized learning skills. Therefore, teachers need to strike a balance between natural strengths and learning styles.

APPROACH TO DIFFERENTIATION OF INSTRUCTION

Tiered Assignments

Tiered activities include a set of related tasks of different levels of complexity. These activities relate to "essential understanding" or critical attributes and key skills that students need to learn. Taking into consideration individual students' needs, teachers assign the activities as alternative means of ensuring that all students learn the concepts of the lesson.

Acceleration/Deceleration

Teachers differentiate instruction by accelerating or decelerating the pace and sequence in which learners move through instruction. Students who demonstrate a high level of mastery can learn the curriculum contents at a faster pace. Struggling students who perform at below grade level need modified activities that allow them to work at a slower pace in order to experience academic success. The depth, breath, and pace of instruction are adjusted by teachers to suit student needs with a strong focus on critical and creative thinking.

Flexible Grouping

Because all students perform at varying levels, the teacher should differentiate instruction through flexible grouping of students. For example, one student may be performing below grade level in math, but at the same time, he or she is above grade level in reading. Therefore, teachers should group highly talented students with those who are below grade level performers. Students should not be allowed to remain in a "static group for any" given subjects "as their learning will accelerate from time to time" (Theroux, P., 2004). It is important to emphasize the point that highly gifted students can gain from participating in flexible grouping. Peer teaching has been supported by research to be very beneficial strategy in a group or cooperative learning for both below and above level students.

> *"When students get used to having a book with them, they make reading a part of their lives."*
> *— Steve Gardiner, 2006*

STRATEGY #10

READING COMPREHENSION STRATEGIES VIA BALANCED LITERACY

There are several strategies that teachers can use to assist students with reading comprehension of fiction and nonfiction texts regardless of the level of complexity. When set in a balanced literacy, these strategies will foster academic achievement for all students whatever their current reading levels are.

- Finding the main idea: The main idea of a reading passage is a sentence that tells what the passage is primarily or mainly about. The main idea question might ask What is the passage mostly about? or What is the main point of this passage? or What is the author trying to tell you?

- Recalling facts and details: There are facts and details in almost every reading passage. The facts and details give more information about the main idea such as who, what, when, where, why, or how. Questions about facts and details are concerned with something that was stated in the passage. To answer a question about facts and details, reread or skim the passage to find the answer. Remember: It is there somewhere.

- Locating the answers: Locating the answers is the most significant reading or test-taking skill that a student can learn. When you don't know the answer right away, go back to the passage and find or locate the information that answers the question. When you are looking for an answer, you are reading for a purpose. This task is like searching for something you have lost. Whenever you are in doubt about the answer, skim the passage quickly, looking for a key word or phrase from the question. Then reread more carefully than you did the first time, looking for the specific fact or detail that answers the question.

- Drawing conclusions: You should know that the author doesn't tell you everything. Therefore, you must "figure out" information on your own because the answers are not stated in the passage. You may have to imagine from what you have read. For example, the sentences might read as follows: The moon cast an eerie glow in Jake's room. Suddenly, he saw a shadow by the window. Frozen with fear, Jake sat up in bed. From the words in the passage, you can figure out that it is nighttime because the moon is out and Jack is in bed. The author further implies that Jake is very scared and can't move. Questions about drawing conclusions often encourage you to read between the lines. You need to make conclusion from what you have read and from what you've seen in you mind.

- Finding word meanings in context: At times when you read, you may find a word of which you do not know the meaning. Often you can tell the meaning of the word by how it is used in the sentence and by the words around it. This method of learning the meaning of new words is referred to as discerning how the word is used in context. Con means "with" and text means "written form." Therefore, you are getting information from the words surrounding the unknown word. Questions about vocabulary words in a passage ask you to decide the meanings of words as they are used in the passage, in context. Remember that the same word can have more than one meaning. Zap the answers that don't make any sense. Next, try each answer that is left in the sentence where the word appears in the passage. Then choose the answer that makes the most sense.

- Understanding sequence: Often times, author presents events or ideas in sequence (see sequence chart above). Various things or events occur at the beginning, middle, and end of a chapter or passage. Questions about sequence ask you to remember and put events or details in a certain order. They often contain key words such as first, then, last, after, or before. Remember that you can look back in the passage to make sure you remember what happened when.

- Recognizing cause and effect: A cause is something that makes something else happens. An effect is the result of a cause. Read this sentence: I forgot to set my alarm clock, so I was late for school. The cause of being late for school was forgetting to set the alarm clock. The effect of forgetting to set the alarm clock was being late for school. Questions about cause and effect usually begin with the key words: why, what happened, or because.

- Making predictions: A prediction or hypothesis is something you think will happen in the future. Questions about predictions ask what will probably or most likely happen next. You will not find direct answers to these questions in the passage. At times, it is helpful to put yourself in a character's place and decide what you would do. There are usually clues in the passage to help you make a good guess about what might happen next.

- Comparing and contrasting: Some questions ask you to find how things are alike or different. This type of question is called "compare and contrast" or finding likenesses and differences. Questions that ask you to compare or contrast usually contain key words such as most like, different, like, similar, or dissimilar.

- Understanding author's purpose: Questions about author's purpose ask you why the author wrote the passage. Most authors write for the following reasons: to persuade (make someone want to do something), to give information, to describe, or to entertain. Use the acronym PIDE to remember the author's purpose. P is for persuade, I is for information, D is for description, and E is for entertain. You might want to write down each of these letters to remind you of the author's purpose.

- Distinguishing between facts and opinion: Questions about facts and opinions ask you to find which statements are "fact statement" and which statements are "opinion statements." A fact is something that is true; it can be proven. An opinion tells how a person feels about something. Remember, facts can be proven, opinions cannot. Facts are usually written in declarative sentences and tell something. Statements that are opinions often contain key words such as most, best, nicest, maybe, some, and greatest or statements that begin with "I think…"
- Interpreting figurative language: Sometimes writers use words in such a way that their meaning is different from their usual dictionary meaning. Poets and authors use common words in a special way and this special language is called "figurative language." By using figurative language, the reader can imagine a scene in a book, the description of a person, or an action by picturing the words in his or her mind. Figures of speech are descriptions that are often fun to visualize. The following are three examples of figurative language:

1. **Simile** – A simile compares two things by using the words *like* or *as.* An example is: He ran as fast as a cheetah. Others are as hard as nails, as strong as an ox, chatters like a monkey, runs like a deer, and as smooth as a glass.

2. **Metaphor** – A metaphor is a direct comparison that compares two things or describes a thing or person as if it were something or someone else without using "like or as." Examples include Ann is a walking encyclopedia, He is faster than a streak of lightning, Dr. Idio's bark is worse than his bite, My new car is a real lemon, or Skip is a clown in class.

3. Personification – Personification happens when a writer gives human qualities to an animal or something else that is NOT human. Emily Dickinson personifies death, portraying it as a man driving a carriage:

> "Because I could not stop for Death-
> He kindly stopped for me-
> The Carriage held but just ourselves-
> And Immortality."

Source: (Adapted from Dr. Judith Shay's handout at reading workshop, Pennington School, 2004)

BALANCE LITERACY

Balance literacy is a reading strategy that focuses on reading, writing, and vocabulary skills. It includes reading to, with, and by children and writing to, with, and by children. Teachers and instructors should model shared reading and writing experiences across curriculum and subject areas. In balance literacy:

- Reading to students enhances their ability to learn sentence structure, develop an understanding of story and text structure, build prediction skills, create mental images, make cognitive connections, and provide them with a strong model of proficient reading in the context of either literature or expository text.

- Reading with students fosters their ability to develop comprehension skills. Teachers should use guided reading sessions specifically to meet the needs of a small group of students in order to help them build basic reading skills and to become proficient and fluent independent readers. Students must be taught how to work in small groups without direct interaction with the teacher.

- Independent reading by students enhances their ability to build self-confidence, fluency, vocabulary, and provides them with opportunities to practice using reading strategies they are learning.

- Writing for and with students gives examples of spelling and mechanics of writing to help foster their understanding of how reading and writing are intertwined or connected. Students can learn to sequence sounds in words.

- Writing by students not only fosters their ability to build confidence as writers, but also it encourages students to learn different types of writing.

Teachers and students can integrate the balance literacy approach across the subject areas such as math, science, or social studies in any grade level. According to Keen's and Zimmerman's *Mosaic of thought* (1997), (as cited in Rutherford, 2002), students should be taught and encouraged to make the following connections based on balance literacy approach:

- Text-to-self connection
- Text-to-text connection
- Text-to-world connection

STRATEGY #11

THREE APPROACHES TO BALANCE LITERACY

- The following chart contains the components of the balance literacy suggested by the Providence Public Schools (PPS), Rhode Island, website (www.providenceschools.org).

Read aloud from all genres – to foster listening and comprehension skills through discussion and writing

Think Aloud - Teach mechanics such as spelling, capitalization, and punctuation

PPS – BALANCE LITERACY METHOD

Literacy Centers – with reading and writing activities across the curriculum

Word Work – to build phonemic awareness or letter-sound relationship and skills

Shared Writing – on various topics in different subject areas

Writer's Workshop – with materials such as pencil, paper, prompts, markers, glue sticks, etc.

Independent Reading – when students read independently with limited teacher supervision

- St. Vrain Valley School District (SVVSD) Balance Literacy Approach in Longmont, Colorado, includes the following components shown in the chart below.

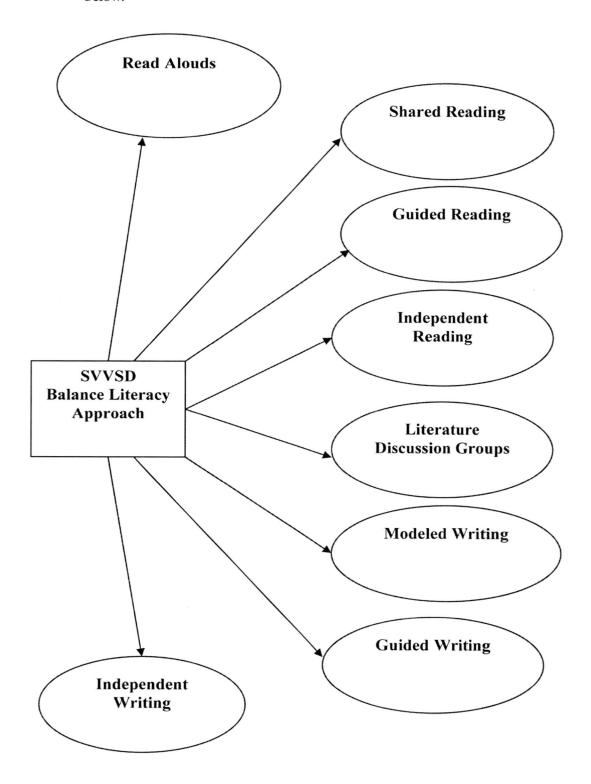

• The McREL Strategic Reading Project used by the Chicago Public Schools suggests the following methods.

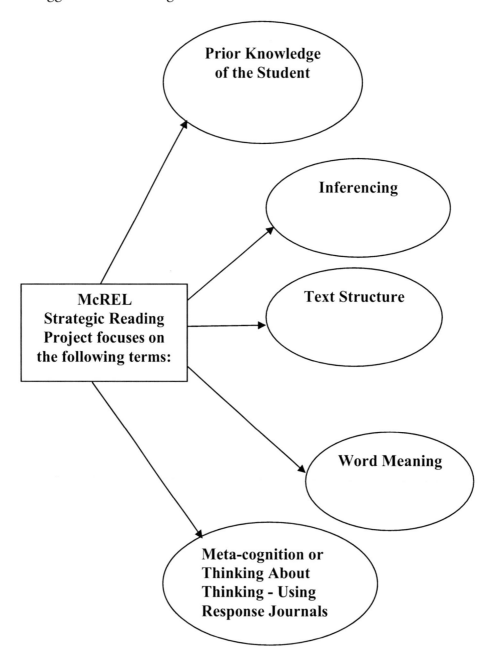

How And What Effective Readers Do

Effective readers:

- Set a purpose for reading
- Access prior knowledge and relate it to new information
- Construct meaning
- Reread, skim, summarize a chapter
- Paraphrase and predict based on chapter headings
- Frame and reframe focused questions before, during and after reading
- Look for important ideas in charts, tables, and graphs
- Test their comprehension of technical information
- Identify patterns in the text that serve as examples of main idea
- Use graphic organizers to organize information
- Sequence events (e.g., in an explanation of historical facts)
- Look for relationships (e.g., between math concepts)
- Mentally execute directions in a manual
- Have a repertoire of strategies and know when to use each
- Think about reading strategies prior to, during, and after reading
- Monitor their understanding of difficult explanations

Source: "A List of Behaviors Practiced by Proficient Readers" from A <u>Review of Literature</u> by Fairfax County Public Schools Secondary Educators: (Adapted from Paula Rutherford, 2002)

What Good Readers Do: From A to Z
(California Reading Association or CRA, 2005)

Proficient readers according to the California Reading Association do the following things prior, during, and after reading:

- A. *"Anticipate the meaning.* They use their prior knowledge and information from the text to make predictions and speculations.
- B. *Become lifelong readers.* By being in the continued presence of reading, writing with parents, teachers, schoolmates, and friends, good readers develop lifelong literacy habits.
- C. *Choose their own reading materials.* From the very early stages, good readers select a variety of books and types of literature to read.

- D. *Do not read every word or attend to every letter.* The more the mind works, the less hard the eyes need to work as good readers focus on larger meaningful pieces of text.
- E. *Elaborate on important parts of the text.* Good readers generate elaboration or embellishment during reading (through summaries, inferences, or note taking, all of which foster greater comprehension, recall, and use of the materials read.
- F. *Focus on fluency by reading.* One of the best ways good readers become fluent is by reading wide range of books.
- G. *Get books.* Good readers go to where books are. They use the library, browse in bookstores, borrow books from friends, and give books as gifts.
- H. *Have a purpose.* Good readers know their reading can be informative, enjoyable, and enriching and a useful tool to solve a variety of problems.
- I. *Imagine when they read.* To facilitate comprehension, good readers make mental pictures when they read.
- J. *Just skim sometimes and judiciously read slowly at other times.* Good readers shift speeds depending on their purpose and the type of books they are reading.
- K. *Know about their mental skills.* Good readers continuously appraise and self-monitor their comprehension as they are reading. They are mega-cognitively aware of what they know, what they want to find out, and how to do that.
- L. *Listen to and enjoy stories and books being read aloud.* An important factor in helping build the background for becoming a good reader is reading aloud to students of all ages.
- M. *Make personal connection with reading.* Good readers make links and applications between the literature and their lives.
- N. *Negotiating meanings by integrating a number of cues or sources of information.* Good readers use and crosscheck four types of cues: their knowledge of the world, oral language (what sounds right), word meaning, and the visual information in the text (letter-sound association).
- O. *Often self-correct.* Good readers use monitoring and problem-solving strategies such as skipping unknown words, rereading, reading ahead, or using an outside source.
- P. Paraphrase Periodically. During reading, good readers put into their own words the gist of what they have been reading.
- Q. *Question.* Good readers ask questions and then read to seek out answers to those questions.
- R. *Respond to literature.* Good readers gradually learn to make internal responses and personal reflections (thoughts and discussions) to literature

by first making a variety of external responses (reconstructions, retellings, redrawings, and rewritings).

- S. *Share with others.* Good readers are always joining together to discuss and share what they are reading with others. Book habits are acquired naturally because of these interactions.
- T. *Take time to read.* Good readers log lots of reading mileage and take advantage of many opportunities in and out of class to read.
- U. *Use prior knowledge.* Good readers use their background experiences.
- V. *Validate predictions.* Good readers verify their predictions as they read. Comprehension equals confirmed predictions.
- W. *Write.* Good readers engage in writing as it relates to reading to enhance both reading and writing ability.
- X. *Expect reading to make sense.* Good readers have a meaning orientation to print, always seeking to make sense when they read.
- Y. *Yearn to read.* Good readers always have a book close by and choose to engage in reading during leisure time. This is a hallmark of a good reader.
- Z. *Zero in on learning strategies when they need them.* As they need strategies and skills to communicate with an author, good readers learn need strategies and skills to communicate with an author in the context of reading" (California Reading Association/CRA).

Source: (A Handout from Guthrie, Fran, Instructional Specialist Team (IST) and Seminar Presenter on "Train for Reading Endurance" PWCS, 2005)

LITERACY RESPONSE STRATEGY

Character Analysis Using Character Web

Teachers can adapt this activity to teach students character analysis after the book has been read in its entirety. The activity can be titled simply

What Am I?

Direction - Select any character from a book you have read. Think about everything you know about the character. Then describe the character as completely as you can by using the character web below.

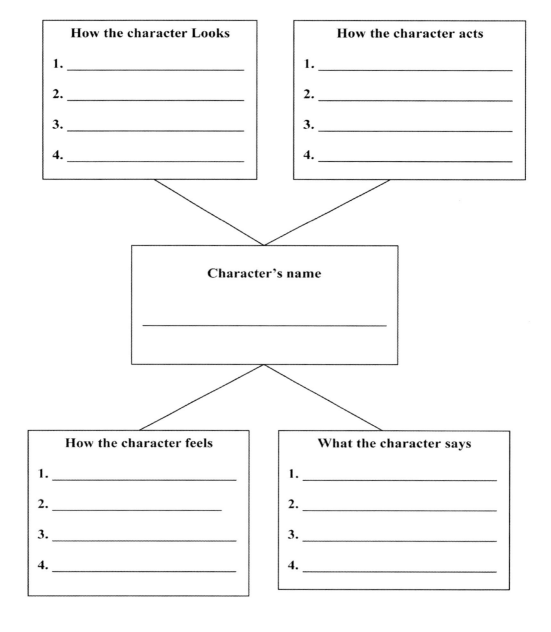

Review Questions For Fiction Texts

Direction – Answer these questions after you have read your story book to the end.

- What do you think is the main idea of this story?
- Write a short description of the main character (s) in your book.
- Write a short statement that describes something in this book that reminds you of another book you have read or any experience you have had similar to the one in this book.
- Compare and contrast two characters in this book or one character to your self to show how you are alike and different.
- Write a summary of this book or story. Make certain that your summary includes the beginning, middle, and ending.
- You can illustrate the book or story.

Write or state

- 3 most important events in the story

- 2 questions you would like to ask the character in the story

- 1 event in this book that reminds you of another book you have read

Samples of Reflective Writing Project: The ABC Book

Direction – Reflect and create an alphabet book to show the concepts you have learned across the curriculum. On page one, you can write a paragraph about anything you have learned this quarter or year that begins with the letter A. You can illustrate the page. Remember, each page must be in alphabetical order. You can write or type your ABC Book. The following are four samples of the ABC Books of fourth graders' reflective writings, excluding their illustrations. The paragraphs are direct quotes followed by the initials of the student's first and last name (see reference list for credits to these students.)

Title: *My ABC Book*

- A. *AFRICAN AMERICANS.* Sadly, African Americans got a bad start in America. They were treated badly during slavery. Many slaves were beaten with whips. If a slave was caught trying to run away, he would be punished by either being killed or having his legs cut off. Many slaves did not know what to do. Finally Harriet Tubman found the Underground railroad and many slaves were free at last.

- B. *BOSTON TEA PARTY.* The Boston Tea Party took place because the settlers were against the taxes. England shipped tea to the settlers and put high taxes on it. The settlers dumped all the tea in the water. While they were doing this, they wore Indian clothes so they wouldn't get caught.

- C. *CHRISTOPHER COLUMBUS.* Christopher Columbus was a man who believed the earth was flat and that if you were to go to the 'end' of it, you'd fall off. He tried a voyage to reach India but landed in St. Augustine. Because he thought he was in India he called the native Americans Indians. When he reached land, he called it The New World we know it as Virginia!

- D. *DIVISION.* Division is a math function that determines how many times a smaller number is in a bigger number. An example is that 5 goes into fifty 10 times. Or 50 divided by 5 equals 10. Sometimes there's a remainder if a number cannot be divided by another number equally. An example of this is 5 goes into fifty-one 10 times with a remainder 1.

- E. *EROSION.* Erosion occurs when the surface of the earth is worn away by the action of water, winds, waves, etc. I've seen erosion on the beach. The waves wash away the sand, especially during high tide.

- F. *FRICTION.* Friction is the rubbing of the surface of one body against that of another. Sometimes friction will cause static electricity. Most of us have had this happen when we wear socks on our feet and rub them against another object, we get chocked by the static electricity caused by friction! Sometimes there's friction between people, like when they don't get along or disagree about something.

- G. *GALLON.* A gallon is a unit of capacity that equals four quarts. Most people buy a gallon of milk at the store. Also … 1 gallon equals 8 pints; I gallon equals 16 cups; 1 gallon equals 128 fluid ounces; 1 gallon equals 3.79liters.

- H. *HARRY FLOOD BYRD*, SR. Harry Flood Byrd, Sr. was the person who invented the "Pay as You Go" system. He was very important in Virginia politics in the mid-twentieth century and wanted limited government. During his term as governor 1926-30, he reorganized and streamlined the state bureaucracy.

- I. *INDIANS.* Indians were actually Native Americans, but when Christopher Columbus arrived in the New World, he thought he was in India. He named the Natives "Indians" by mistake but the name stuck. Chief Powhatan was chief of many tribes. Indians made their own weapons from natural resources like wood, animals, and rocks. They lived off the land.

- J. *JAMESTOWN.* The fourth grade took a really fun field trip to Jamestown! We learned that only men came over to Jamestown at first in order to get settled. Women soon followed, along with slavery, taxes, and battles. Some houses were made of wattle- and-daub and were topped with thatched roofs – like James Fort. They were well built, but a fire could destroy them quickly.

- K. *KING GEORGE III.* King George III was not a popular king because he wanted to control everything. He made very poor decisions while he was ruler. At one point the King invited his former critic, William Pitt, to form a new government. George now used all the powers he had to help Pitt maintain control of Parliament. This made the king unpopular with the Whigs, a group who favored fewer powers for the monarchy. In 1810 his insanity became permanent and he died in 1820.

- L. *LIFEWORK.* We had lifework every night! Lifework is important because it helps us remember what we learned during the day. If our lifework wasn't done, we had to finish it outside during recess. Most other schools call this type of work "homework" but Pennington calls it "lifework" because our life depends on it! To exceed expectations, do you lifework!

- M. *METAPHOR.* A metaphor is a figure of speech in which a term or phrase is applied to something to which it is not literally applicable in order to suggest a resemblance. A couple good examples of a metaphor are It's a dog's life. Computers are the vehicles of tomorrow.

- N. *NOUN.* A noun is a person, place, or thing. Some examples are: person: mother, doctor; Place: church, beach; Thing: jacket, phone.

- O. *OCTAGON.* An octagon is a shape that has right angles and eight sides. I find it easy to remember how many sides it has because an octopus has eight legs and an octagon has eight sides!

- P. *PRIDE.* Pride is an important character trait at Pennington. We are taught to take pride in our work and ourselves and it's important that we always do. Pride means being proud of yourself and acting in a way that will make you proud to be you.

- Q. *QUEEN ELIZABETH I.* Queen Elizabeth I accomplished a lot during her reign. Literature was very successful and her religious compromise made many people comfortable. Fashion and education became very popular because of Elizabeth's knowledge, good behavior, and style.

- R. *ROANOKE ISLAND.* The first English Colony of Roanoke started with only 100 householders and was founded in 1885. This happened 22 years before Jamestown and 37 years before the Pilgrims landed in Massachusetts. Sir Walter Raleigh was in charge and in 1584 he was granted a patent by Queen Elizabeth I to colonize America. The colony lasted 10 months.

- S. *SUSAN CONSTANT.* Susan Constant was the largest of the three ships led by Captain Christopher Newport. His voyage in 1607 found the first permanent English settlement in North America. It was Jamestown in the new colony of Virginia. On that voyage Susan Constant carried 71 colonists.

- T. *TIDEWATER.* The Tidewater region is the far east area of Virginia. It is bordered by the Potomac on the north, the Chesapeake Bay on the east, North Carolina on the south, and the Fall line on the west. The important rivers are the Rappahannock, the York, the James, and the Potomac. The eastern shore of Virginia is a peninsula that is separated from the rest of the Tidewater by the Chesapeake Bay. The weather in this region is mild and land is a coastal plain.

- U. *UNITED STATES OF AMERICA.* The capital of the United States of America is Washington, D.C. There are 50 states. Forty-eight states are together in North America, Alaska is connected to Western Canada, and Hawaii is made up of several islands in the Pacific Ocean.

- V. *VIOLIN.* The violin is a bowed stringed musical instrument that has four strings tuned a perfect fifth apart. The range of the violin is from the G just below middle C to the highest notes of the piano. It is the smallest and highest- tuned number of violin family of string instruments, which also includes the viola and cello. A person who plays violin is called a violinist or fiddler.

- W. *WASHINGTON, D.C.* Washington, D.C. is the capital city of the United States of America. "D.C." stands for the District of Columbia. The city is named after George Washington who was the first president of the United States. A lot of people call it "the District," D.C., or just Washington. There are many museums and monuments in D.C. The White House is where the President lives, and the Washington Monument is the tallest building in D.C.

- X. *EX'-PRESIDENTS.* George Washington was the first President and George W. Bush is the current President. In between these two Georges were 41 other presidents. So far there are 42 ex-presidents of the United States!

- Y. *YARD* A yard is a unit of measurement that is equal to 3 feet. A yardstick is 3 feet long. Football fields are measured by yards and football games use yards like 1st down and 10 to go.
- Z. *ZERO.* Zero is a number measuring 'nothing' and comes before the number one. It looks like this: 0. If you add 0 to a number, the number doesn't change. If you multiply a number by 0, the answer is always 0. (R.E., 2006).

Title: *My End-of-The-Year ABC Book*

- A. *A is for Abolitionist.* An abolitionist is a person against slavery. They (he/she) also worked to end it. Most abolitionists were from the north. John Brown is an abolitionist. He led a revolt in a federal arsenal. That shows that abolitionists took risky sacrifices.
- B. *B is for Boston Tea Party.* The Boston Tea party took place in 1773. Where a group of patriots dressed as (like) Indians and dumped all the British tea in the water. The water looked liked a big teapot. That's why we call it the Boston Tea party. The British punished Boston and closed their ports. The punishment hurts Boston a lot.
- C. *C is for Camouflage.* Camouflage is an adaptation which allows someone to hide from its predators. You can only camouflaged by color. A praying (preying) mantis is green, so it would blend into a leaf. But animals aren't the only ones that use camouflage. Armies do too, so they won't be seen by the enemy. Camouflage is a great advantage.
- D. *D is for Debt.* Being in debt means to owe someone something. Sometimes being in debt is bad. You can owe someone 3000 dollars and you only have 2000 dollars. A credit card is something that can put you in debt. During the Reconstruction period Virginia was deeply in debt.
- E. *E is for Equation.* An equation is a problem that uses the equals sign (=), addition sign (+), subtraction sign (−), etc. Another word for equation is number sentence. If you are adding, all the numbers before the equal sign are called addends. Equations can be as long as you want. You can add, subtract, multiply, etc.
- F. *F is for Fraction.* A fraction is a part of a whole. There are two parts to a fraction, a numerator, which is the top number and the denominator, which is the bottom number. The denominator is always larger than the numerator. If this doesn't happen to a fraction then it is improper. You can change an improper fraction to a mixed number which has a whole number with it. But you can also change a mixed number into an improper fraction.
- G. *G is for Graphs.* Graphs are a major way to show data. An example of a graph is a line graph. A line graph is a graph that shows data in time. A

pie graph is a graph that shows data that can be sorted in percentage (or fraction). Graphs are used in businesses, science projects, conventions, etc.

- H. *H is for House of Burgesses.* The House of burgesses was the first elected legislative body in America. This legislative body was formed in 1619. This group represented Virginia. Soon the house of Burgesses was named the General Assembly. And which is still in the legislative branch of our government.

- I. *I is for Independence.* Independence means to be free. An example of the opposite is when British didn't give Americans the right to do things they wanted. That is what led to the Revolutionary War. The slaves were also given independence but not after the Civil War. Independence is very important to America.

- J. *J is for Jim Crow Laws.* Jim Crow Laws were the laws that had negative effect on African Americans. These laws separated whites and blacks from using public facilities. Jim Crow laws also led to the Civil Rights Movement in which Dr. Martin Luther King, Jr. led. African Americans and some whites boycotted and did what they could to help stop the Jim Crow Laws from continuing.

- K. *K is for Kinetic Energy.* Kinetic energy is energy in motion. Potential energy is the opposite. It is energy in rest. Kinetic energy is anything you do while moving and using force. You can use kinetic energy in recess and outside.

- L. *L is for Lever.* A lever is a simple machine. It has 3 classes. The 1st class lever has the fulcrum in the middle and the load and effort force on the other 2 sides. The 2nd class lever has the load in the middle and the effort force and fulcrum on the other 2 sides. The 3rd class lever has the effort force in the middle and the fulcrum and load on the other 2 sides. A lever is very helpful.

- M. *M is for Mode.* Mode is the number that occurs the most frequently. In the set of number (3, 4, 7, 9, 9, 9, 6, 3), 9 is the mode. Mode can also be classified as cluster.

- N. *N is for Nucleus.* Nucleus is the middle of a molecule. In the nucleus there are protons and neutrons. The electrons orbit the nucleus.

- O. *O is for Outcome.* An outcome is the result. What comes out in the end is another way to say it. If I make a pattern the one that comes next is the outcome. We usually say outcome in science or math.

- P. *P is for Pulley.* A pulley is another simple machine. It is used to lift things up. There are three kinds of pulley. Fixed, movable, and fixed and movable pulley. They are all used in different ways.

- Q. *Q is for Quotient.* A quotient is the answer to a division problem. It can be even with no remainder or opposite. The quotient can only have a remainder less than a divisor. You can also make it a decimal.
- R. *R is for Radius.* The radius of a circle would be from the middle (center) of the circle to its circumference. A circumference is the outside of a circle. There is also a chord. It is a line that connects two points on the circumference of a circle.
- S. "*S is for Simile.* A simile is a figure of speech that compares 2 things using "like" or "as." For example, My dog is quick as a cheetah. While a metaphor is almost the same. An example is "My dog is my lifeguard." In a simile and metaphor you have to interpret what it means.
- T. *T is for Tobacco.* Tobacco was a cash crop in Virginia for a long time. That means it was used for money than for pleasure (household consumption). Tobacco was famous and was a source of wealth. One day it became not so popular anymore.
- U. *U is for Ulysses S. Grant.* Ulysses grant was a union general. He was a strong army leader. He defeated Robert E. Lee and his force. Robert E. Lee even surrendered to him in Appomattox Courthouse. That really made him famous.
- V. *V is for Voltage.* Voltage is a measurement in which negative charges flow. The unit of voltage is volt. Scientists sometimes use it too.
- W. W is for Weight. Weight is a measurement of how heavy or light something is. It is usually expressed in ounces and pounds. A scale can measure people and items.
- X. *X is for X-axis.* X axis (axes) are found in coordinate grids. There is a y axis. There is a negative and positive x axis. There is also a negative and positive y axis.
- Y. *Y is for Yorktown.* Yorktown was the turning point of the Revolutionary War. It's where General Cornwallis surrendered to the patriots. Yorktown is also located along the York River.
- Z. *Z is for Zero.* Zero is a number. If you add a number to zero you get the same thing. If you divide by zero you get zero. If you multiply by zero you get zero (A. L., 2006).

Title: *My ABC Book*

- A. *A for Astronomy.* Astronomy is the study of stars and planets. An example is the solar system and constellation.
- B. *B for Benjamin Franklin.* Ben Franklin discovered electricity. He did that with his famous kite experiment. He invented the lightning rod and the first volunteer fire department (V.F.D).

- C. *C for Confederate States.* The Confederate States formed because the northern states (Union) wanted no slavery and the Confederate States (southern states) wanted to keep their slaves. The country then split apart by north to south.
- D. *D for Decimals.* A decimal is another way to write a fraction. There are columns to show you the place value. An example of a decimal is 3.48 which mean three and forty-eight hundredths.
- E. *E for Ecosystem.* An ecosystem is the living and nonliving things in an environment. Examples are animals, plants, and rocks.
- F. *F for Fractions.* Fractions are another way to write decimal. (See letter D). Fractions are parts of a whole. Fractions can be converted and made into a mixed number.
- G. *G for George Washington.* George Washington was the first president. He also was commander in-chief in the Revolutionary War. George Washington is known for being a great leader. He is an inspiration to other presidents.
- H. *H for Harry Flood Byrd, Sr.* Harry Flood Byrd, Sr. was governor. He thought of the "pay as you plan." At one point, the Supreme Court stated that all public schools must be integrated. But Harry didn't like it. He then started the "massive resistance" plan so all schools either stay segregated or they won't get money to support the school.
- I. *I for Iroquoian.* Iroquoian was an Indian language group. They used to live in central Virginia.
- J. *J for Jamestown.* The James River is important because it led the colonists to the first permanent settlement called Jamestown.
- K. *K for Kinetic Energy.* Kinetic energy is energy in motion. It is the opposite of potential energy. Examples of kinetic energy are rolling down a hill or marble rolling across the table.
- L. *L for line graph.* A line graph is a graph to tell how the subject changes over time.
- M. *M for Manassas.* Manassas was the place where the first war was held during the Civil War. General Thomas Jackson got his name here. His nickname is "Stonewall." Manassas is also where our school is located.
- N. *N for Negative Charges.* Negative charges are the opposite of positive charges. Negative charges form when positive charges are knocked off a material making it negative.
- O. *O for Obtuse Angle.* Obtuse angles are greater than right angle. Obtuse angles are the widest type of angles. Other angles are right and acute angles.
- P. *P for Potential Energy.* Potential energy is the opposite of kinetic energy (see k). Potential energy is energy that is not in motion.

- Q. *Q for Quotient.* A quotient is the answer to a division problem. A quotient is the opposite of a product. An example of a quotient is $4 \div 2 = 2$. The 2 on the right side of the equal sign is the quotient.
- R. *R for Robert E. Lee.* Robert E. Lee was a general for the south. He was the one who surrendered to Ulysses S. Grant at Appomattox Courthouse.
- S. *S for "Stonewall" Jackson.* Stonewall Jackson's real name is Thomas Jackson. His nickname is "Stonewall." He got his name because it was told that he and his troop just stood in one place looking like stonewall.
- T. *T for Treaty.* A treaty is a document to declare peace between each other. The Indians and the colonists signed treaties.
- U. *U for Ulysses Grant.* Ulysses S. Grant was a general of the north. General Robert E. Lee surrendered to him.
- V. *V for Volume.* You can find volume in 3-D shapes. To find volume, you can multiply length times width times height. Then you found volume of the figure. The answer is written in cubic unit.
- W. *W for Weather.* Weather changes in the year. Types of weather are sunny, rainy, cloudy, snowy, and other things you see on the news.
- X. *X for X-Rays.* X-Rays are machines (photos) that check if you have a broken bone. They help you see the bone without needing to cut the body open.
- Y. *Y for Yorktown.* Yorktown is where the last war (battle) of the Revolutionary War was fought. That is where Brittan (Britain) surrendered.
- Z. *Z for Zero Property.* Zero property is when you add, subtract, multiply, or divide zero with a different number, then you would get 0 or other number you need (C.G., 2006).

Title: *Mike's ABC Book*
- A. *Arthur Ashe Junior.* He was the first African American to win the U.S. Tennis Championship and Wimbledon. He also worked for fair and equal treatment for all people.
- B. *Blue Ridge Mountains.* This is a mountain range in the Eastern part of the Appalachians that stretches from Pennsylvania to Georgia.
- C. *Chesapeake Bay.* The Chesapeake Bay is an Inlet of the Atlantic Ocean and partly enclosed by the states of Maryland and Virginia. It is where the colonists first arrived. It is also part of the Coastal Plain.
- D. *Declaration of Independence.* The Declaration of Independence is a document officially declaring that the American colonists are free from Great Britain to form a new nation. It was signed by 27 men. John Hancock wrote the first signature and it is the biggest (longest) one. Without this document, we would still be British.

- E. *Eastern Shore.* The Eastern Shore is a peninsular between the Atlantic Ocean and the Chesapeake Bay. It is shared by Maryland and Virginia.
- F. *Fredericksburg.* Fredericksburg is an independent city on the Rappahannock River at the edge of Piedmont. It is also the site of a major battle in 1812.
- G. *Germany.* Germany is a central European nation between France and Poland. Its present territory stretches from the Alps to the North and to the Baltic Sea. They helped the United States during the Revolutionary War.
- H. *Henry Patrick.* Patrick Henry was a member of the House of Burgesses. He convinced the people that they should break away from England. He did this by saying: 'Give me liberty of give me death!
- I. *Industries.* Industries are very important to Virginia. They use machines to replace human labor. Some examples are fishing and ship building. Without them, our economy would go down.
- J. *Jamestown.*   Jamestown was founded in 1607. It was also our first capital. 1620 first saw the arrival of women and Africans to Jamestown..
- K. *King George III.* King George III was the king of England who sent settlers to America by signing a charter.
- L. *Legislative Branch.* The Legislative Branch is one of the three branches of the United States government. It is the one that makes the laws.
- M. *Manassas.* I live in this city which is in the state of Virginia. There were two great battles here during the Civil War. They were called the First and Second Battles of Manassas.
- N. *Niche.* A niche is an animal's job, a cycle they go through. It is something they use to protect themselves.
- O. *Octagon.* An octagon is a shape with eight sides. The word octa means eight in Greek. That is how it got its name.
- P. *Pentagon.* A pentagon is a shape with five sides. The military building called the pentagon (… has five sides), was attacked by terrorists in 2001. I still don't know why terrorists would attack a shape.
- Q. *Quotient.* A quotient is the answer to a division problem.
- R. *Rhombus.* A rhombus is a parallelogram with equal sides. One of them is a square.
- S. *Social Studies.* Social studies is a subject that we study in school. There is also a history of the state of Virginia in our social studies book.
- T. *Turner*, Nat. Nat Turner was an abolitionist (who was actually a slave). He led a rebellion of the slaves against plantation owners.
- U. *Ulysses S. Grant.* Ulysses S. Grant was a Union General during the Civil War, fighting with the North against the South. He was also an abolitionist.

- V. Virginia. Virginia is the state I live in. It was settled by colonists in 1607. The first female ever born (to the colonists) in Virginia was named the queen of England because she was called the 'Virgin Queen.
- W. *Williamsburg*. Williamsburg was the capital of Virginia during the Revolutionary War. The Governor's Palace is there and that is where the governor of Virginia and his family lived. It is also the second capital of Virginia.
- X. *Xylophone*. Xylophone is an instrument with metal plates in different lengths that you strike with a stick. It is like a primitive piano.
- Y. *Yorktown*. Yorktown is where the last battle of the Revolutionary War was fought. It is in the state of Virginia. George Washington led the American revolutionaries to victory in the year 1781.
- Z. *Zero*. Zero is a special number. When you multiply by 10's you can just add a zero to the end of the original number. For example, if you multiply 5 X 10, you get 50 (M. M., 2006)

The above samples of students' reflective writings provide a unique opportunity for the teacher to understand the knowledge base and thinking process of the students. Reflective writing is a powerful tool for teaching and learning for teachers and student alike.

PROFESSIONAL DEVELOPMENT

Professional development is defined here as consistent, on-the-job personnel training that is directed at wide range of skills, abilities, strengths, and needs which are identified through clinical supervision and evaluation of instructional staff. The purpose of professional development should be to enhance school effectiveness, improve teaching skills, improve student achievement, and increase staff morale. Professional development can take the form of inservice, workshops, and seminars. Regardless of what format it takes, a professional development program should revolve around the premise that the participants are adult learners. The professional development model adopted by a school or school district should be based on adults learning theory, which is a research-based model.

The Adults learning Theory ("Andragogy") Model

The adults learning theory model (attributed to Malcolm Knowles), is often defined as the "science of andragogy." That is, it is the art of helping adults learn because research has shown that adults are self-directed learners, and they draw from their experiences (Idio, 2004).

In adults learning theory model, the trainer (presenter) assumes the role of a facilitator; he or she involves the participants (teachers) in the process of determining the training elements. The process is referred to as andragogical process design. The adults learning theory model of professional development program has the following characteristics:

- Climate setting
- Involving learners in mutual planning
- Involving learners in formulating their learning objectives
- Involving learners in designing plans
- Helping learners in evaluating their learning plans and outcomes
- Involving learners in their learning

Self-direction has become the foundation of the methodology of andragogy, which makes the experience of the learner to supercede the experience of the presenter. Galbo (1998) cited Diana Dempwolf's work, which suggested the following approaches for professional development programs. Staff development program should:

- Use lectures only for conveying information
- Use demonstrations for instructional strategies
- Provide opportunities for guided practices
- Use case study
- Provide opportunities for self-directed learning
- Provide opportunities for trying and discussing new strategies among colleagues
- Provide opportunities for peer coaching
- Elicit support from building administrators who will be willing to tolerate mistakes as teachers (learners) implement new strategies

In specifying the critical components of adults learning theory, Galbo (1998) cited Specks' (1996) suggestions which show that:

- Adults need real-world applications; the training will be more meaningful to the participants if they can use what they have learned in their work places (classrooms).
- Adults want to be treated as competent professionals; participants need some control over the specifics of what, why, when, and where details of their learning.
- Adult learning involves egos; professional development opportunities should be structured to allow support from colleagues and to reduce the fear from judgment when teachers (participants) are learning to apply new skills.
- Adults need constructive feedback on their efforts to learn new skills.

- Adults benefit from professional development activities that allow them to participate in small group activities that provide opportunities for application, analysis, synthesis, and evaluation.
- Adult learners are unique individuals with a wide range of skills and experiences; individual needs and experiences must be accommodated in the professional development planning and implementation.
- The transfer of learning must be facilitated "Coaching and other kinds of follow-up support must be provided to help adult learners transfer learning into daily practice so that it is sustained" (Galbo, 1998).

The 20 Key Elements of Effective Professional Development Program (Idio, 2004)

In designing a professional development program, school administrators and human resources developers should consider the following elements:

- Increasing participant learning is the overarching goal of all training.
- The school is the unit of change.
- Professional development is an ongoing process, not one-shot approach.
- All educators should be life-long learners.
- The involvement and support of the administrator is a key factor.
- Setting and working toward improvement of goals should involve the teachers and staff of the school.
- Improvement efforts must recognize the values, norms, and beliefs that shape the school culture and practice.
- Policies and practices must be connected to the change process.
- Ownership or commitment is gained through input.
- The primary goal of professional development activities is school improvement, but both school and individual growth must be addressed in the effort.
- School district must provide resources to schools for this purpose.
- Planning and implementation should adopt adult learning theory.
- Coaching and ongoing systematic support are required for the transfer of learning from training into applied daily practice in the classroom.
- Schools should provide recognition and rewards for those involved in efforts to grow professionally.
- Teachers and other stakeholders must share decision about time, schedule, curriculum (content), personnel, space, and materials.
- Professional development should support instructional and program development.

- Educators must have opportunities to learn from and collaborate with colleagues.
- Opportunities should be provided in schools for discussions (reflections) most preferably at staff and grade level meetings.
- Participation across job function (role) will increase shared understanding, etc.
- Broader support mechanisms outside the school are needed, such as networks, collaborations, coalitions, and partnerships with individuals and groups outside the schools.

By integrating the above research-based professional development elements into professional development program, teachers develop stronger voices to present their perspectives, learn to exercise leadership with their colleagues, use their first-hand experience to create new possibilities for all students through collaborative work, and develop a community of shared understanding that enriches their teaching and provide a level of instruction that will promote student learning and eventually close the achievement gaps among students subgroups (Idio, 2006).

TECHNOLOGY INTEGRATION

As teachers are beginning to develop confidence about integrating technology into instructional process in the classroom, it is equally important for school districts and administrators to provide greater support for teachers in learning to use technology effectively in the classroom. Technology is a tool that teachers can use to change the way they teach. Technology integration in the curriculum can improve students' learning processes and outcomes; it can enhance teachers' ability to utilize interactive multimedia and telecommunications technologies in instructional process. When teachers create a project-based learning, students are engaged in their learning. Therefore, putting technologies in the hands of our teachers and students in the classrooms will create equitable use for all students, and ultimately, no child will be left behind. With adequate training and support, teachers can integrate technology in the classroom by using it:

- To assess classroom learning
- To plan instructions
- For presentations
- To accelerate core curricula subjects such as reading, math, science, social studies, and geography
- To support the application of concept maps and graphics in teaching and learning
- To reinforce states and federal standards
- For communication with colleagues, students, and parents

- To conduct research projects
- To access research-based best practices and instructional strategies

The Impact of Equitable Use of Education Technology

When it comes to making a decision by a school or district to integrate <u>education technology</u> into the curriculum, one of its goals should be to establish plans and policies for all students to have <u>equitable access and use</u>. That means setting aside appropriate funding for professional development and support for teachers. When teachers become proficient in the use and integration of technology, they will use the technologies effectively in teaching the curriculum for the benefit of all students in the classroom.

According to the National Academy of Sciences and the National Academy of Engineering Studies technology in the classrooms plays a significant role in promoting educational opportunities for all students (1995). They believe

"Technology deployed in education can help remove inequities between the schools of the inner city and the suburbs, between cities and rural districts.... Technology can become the force that equalizes the educational opportunities of all children regardless of location and social and economic circumstance."

To paraphrase Gabe and Gabe (1996), as cited in "Critical Issue," he reported that educational technology can provide equal learning opportunities in many ways. For example, telecommunications allow access to people through electronic mail and bulletin boards, access to interactive services through on-line discussion groups, interactive conferences, interactive tutorials, access to files through on-line databases, library holdings on a local or campuswide network, and text and graphic files on the Internet ("Critical Issue ..."1996)

Means and Olson (1995), as cited in "Critical Issue," noted that educational technology at school can provide access to students from low-income homes, where there is limited or no access to technology, "a needed edge to compete with children coming from more affluent homes, where technology is commonplace." Guaranteeing access for all classrooms to affordable education technology in order to achieve curricular goals, makes it possible to begin to address the inequities that exist among schools and districts in the availability of instructional resources. Teachers must be skilled enough to engage students in "technology-supported" and "project-based" instruction by integrating technologies into several curriculum subjects ("Critical Issue ..." 1996).

> *"Testing has become a fixture in every classroom;*
> *teachers stop whining and get on with it."*
> *~ (Dr. Ignatius E. Idio, 2006)*

CHAPTER 2
Assessment of Classroom Learning

State Standards and No Child Left Behind (NCLB) Mandates

Whether we like it or not, testing is here to stay, if not permanently, but for a foreseeable future. In addition to the states' standards, the federal government also mandates states and local school districts to assess classroom learning to determine if students are learning what the teachers are teaching in our classrooms. Therefore, chapter 2 will attempt to address these three questions. *Why should we assess student learning?*

Do students really learn the specific curricular objectives that teachers are teaching them? How do teachers and instructors know whether or not students are really learning and mastering the concepts that they are teaching?

Assessment of classroom learning is necessary because of the following rationales:

- The mandates of No Child Left Behind (NCLB) Act of 2002.
- Diagnostic purposes
- Formative assessment
- Summative assessment
- Impact on teaching and learning
- Standardized test

The NCLB:

- Testing: Mandates Annual testing of all students in grades 3-12
- Adequate yearly progress (AYP): Mandates that states and school districts must demonstrate each year that an additional percentage of all students have reached the proficient level
- Reporting: Mandates that states and schools districts must issue report cards to parents and the general public that describe how every group of students has performed on the assessment

The National Center for Educational Statistics (NCES) 2005 Assessment Results

The 2005 NCES Assessment Results show interesting trends. In both the short and long term investigations of reading and mathematic performances for grades 4 and 8, the National Center for Educational Statistics NCES) reported the following scores for both the national and states progress.

The short-term national reading results (NAEP/NCES, 2005)

- On a 0 to 500 point scale, fourth-graders' average score was 1 point higher and eighth-graders' average score was 1 point lower in 2005 than in 2003. Average scores in 2005 were 2 points higher than in the first assessment year, 1992, at both grades 4 and 8. (See Charts A&B below).
- Between 1992 and 2005, there was no significant change in the percentage of fourth-graders performing at or above Basic, but the percentage performing at or above Proficient increased during this time.

The percentage of eighth-graders performing at or above *Basic* was
   higher in 2005 (73 percent) than in 1992 (69 percent), but there was no significant change in the percentage scoring at or above *Proficient* between these same years.

Reading results for states (NAEP/NCES, 2005)

- Examining the short-term changes between 2003 and 2005, when all 50 states, the District of Columbia, and Department of Defense (DoD) schools were assessed, results showed mixed outcomes for grades 4 and 8. At grade 4, average scores increased in 7 states and in the DoD schools and decreased in 2 states. The percentage of students performing at or above Basic increased in 3 states and in the DoD schools and decreased in 2 states.
- At grade 8, no state had a higher average score in 2005 than in 2003, and 7 states had lower scores. The percentage of students performing at or above Basic increased in 1 state and decreased in 6 states.

The long-term reading results (NAEP/NCES, 2005)

- Turning to the longer trends at grade 4, there were 42 states and jurisdictions that participated in both 1992 and 2005. The District of Columbia and 19 states had higher average scores and 3 states had lower average scores in 2005 than in 1992. Over the same period, the percentage of students performing at or above *Basic* increased in 15 states and decreased in 3 states.
- At grade 8, the first state assessment was given in 1998 in 38 states and jurisdictions. Three states had higher average scores in 2005 compared to 1998, and 8 states had lower average scores. The percentage of students

performing at or above *Basic* increased in 3 states and in the DoD schools and decreased in 11 states.

Reading Results for Student Groups at Grade 4 (**NAEP/NCES, 2005**)

- The average scores for White, Black, Hispanic, and Asian/Pacific Islander students increased between 1992 and 2005. Looking at the short-term trend, Black and Hispanic students each scored higher on average in 2005 than in 2003. The White-Black and White-Hispanic score gaps narrowed during this same time.
- Students who were eligible for free or reduced-price school lunch and those who were not eligible had higher average scores in 2005 than in 1998. In the short term, students who were eligible showed a 2-point increase from 2003 to 2005.
- In 2005, female students scored higher on average than male students. Male students' average score increased by 3 points from 1992 to 2005. (See Chart C below).

Reading Results for Student Groups at Grade 8 (NAEP/NCES, 2005)

- White, Black, and Hispanic students scored higher, on average, in 2005 than in 1992.
- The average score for students who were not eligible for free or reduced-price lunch decreased by 1 point between 2003 and 2005. The longer trend between 1998 and 2005 showed no statistically significant changes regardless of free-lunch eligibility.
- Both male and female students' average scores showed decreases between 2003 and 2005. In the longer term, the average score for male students was 3 points higher in 2005 than in 1992.

CHART A shows Average reading scale scores, grade 4:
Various years, 1992–2005 (NCES, 2005)

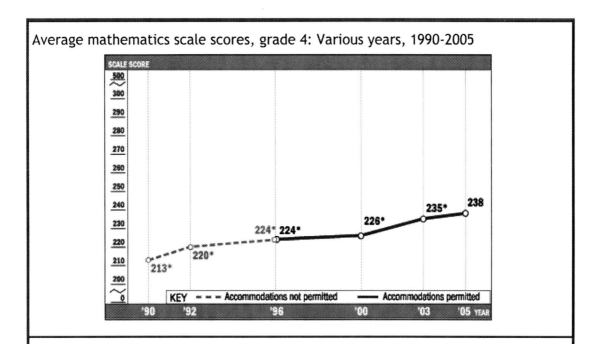

Average mathematics scale scores, grade 4: Various years, 1990-2005

<u>Significantly different</u> from 2005.
NOTE: The dashed and solid lines represent results based on administrations when <u>accommodations</u> were not permitted and when accommodations were permitted, respectively.

Source: Adapted from National Canter for Educational Statistics (NCES, 2005)

CHART B shows Average reading scale scores, grade 8:
Various years,1992–2005 (NCES, 2005).

- The national average grade 8 reading score was 2 points higher in 2005 than in 1992 but 1 point lower than in 2003.

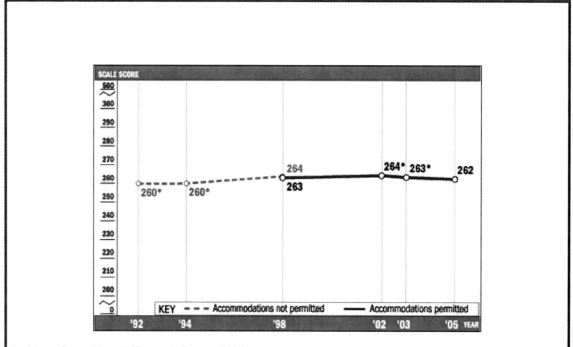

* <u>Significantly different</u> from 2005.
NOTE: The dashed and solid lines represent results based on administrations when <u>accommodations</u> were not permitted and when accommodations were permitted, respectively.

Source: Adapted from National Canter for Educational Statistics (NCES, 2005)

CHART C shows Average scale scores in reading,
by gender, grade 4: Various years, 1992–2005 (NCES, 2005)

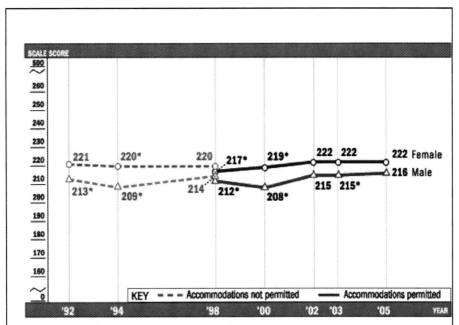

* <u>Significantly different</u> from 2005.
NOTE: The dashed and solid lines represent results based on
administrations when <u>accommodations</u> were not permitted
and when accommodations were permitted, respectively.

Source: Adapted from National Canter for Educational Statistics (NCES, 2005)

National Mathematics Results (NCES, 2005)

- Mathematics performance Improved for the nation, for the majority of states, and for many student groups. Fourth-graders' average score was three points higher and eighth-graders' average score was one point higher in 2005 than in 2003, on a 0 to 500 point scale. The average scores increased since the first assessment year, 1990, by 25 points at grade 4 and by 16 points at grade 8. (See Charts D&E below).

- Between 1990 and 2005, the percentage of fourth-graders performing at or above Basic increased by 30 percentage points, from 50 to 80 percent, and the percentage performing at or above Proficient increased from 13 to 36 percent. The percentage of eighth-graders performing at or above Basic was 17 percentage points higher in 2005 (69 percent) than in 1990 (52 percent), and the percentage performing at or above Proficient increased from 15 to 30 percent.

Mathematics Results for the States (NCES, 2005)

- Examining the short-term trends between 2003 and 2005, when all 50 states and the District of Columbia and Department of Defense Schools were assessed, results show average scores for students at grade 4 increased in 31 states and both jurisdictions. The percentage of students performing at or above *Basic* increased in 23 states and the District of Columbia.

- At grade 8, there were seven states with higher average scores in 2005 than in 2003. The percentage of students performing at or above *Basic* increased in 5 states.

- Turning to the longer trend, the first state assessment at grade 4 was given in 1992 in 42 states and jurisdictions. Each of them had a higher average score and a greater percentage of students performing at or above *Basic* in 2005 than in 1992.

- At grade 8, there were 38 states and jurisdictions that participated in both 1990 and 2005. Each of them had a higher average score and a greater percentage of students performing at or above Basic in 2005 than in 1990.

Mathematics Results for Student Groups at Grade 4 (NCES, 2005)

- White fourth-graders scored higher on average in mathematics than their Black and Hispanic peers in 2005. The average scores for all three of these racial/ethnic groups were higher in 2005 than in any previous assessment year.

- In 2005, students who were eligible for free or reduced-price school lunch and those who were not eligible had higher average scores in 2005 than in 1996.

- In 2005, male students scored higher on average than female students. Both male and female fourth-graders' average scores were higher in 2005 than in any previous assessment year.

Mathematics Results for Student Groups at Grade 8 (NCES, 2005)

- The average scores for White, Black, and Hispanic eighth-graders were higher in 2005 than in any previous assessment year.
- Students who were eligible for free or reduced-price lunch and those who were not eligible scored higher on average in 2005 than in any previous assessment year when information on eligibility was collected, from 1996 through 2003.
- Average scores for male and female eighth-graders were both higher in 2005 than in 1990 or in 2003.
- The national average mathematics score at grade 8 showed a 1-point increase between 2003 and 2005 and was 16 points higher in 2005 than in 1990. (See Chart E below).

CHART D shows Average Mathematics Scale
Scores for the Nation at Grade 4 (NCES, 2005).

• The national average mathematics score at grade 4 increased by 3 points from
  2003 to 2005 and by 25 points from 1990 to 2005.

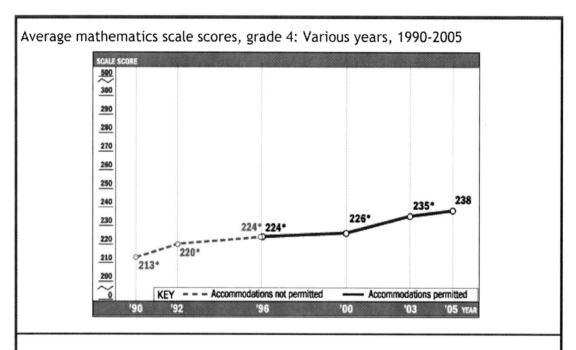

Average mathematics scale scores, grade 4: Various years, 1990-2005

<u>Significantly different</u> from 2005.
NOTE: The dashed and solid lines represent results based on
administrations when <u>accommodations</u> were not permitted and when
accommodations were permitted, respectively.

Source: Adapted from National Canter for Educational Statistics (NCES, 2005)

CHART E shows Average Mathematics Scale
Scores for the Nation at Grade 8 (NCES, 2005).

- The national average mathematics score at grade 8 showed a 1-point increase between 2003 and 2005 and was 16 points higher in 2005 than in 1990.

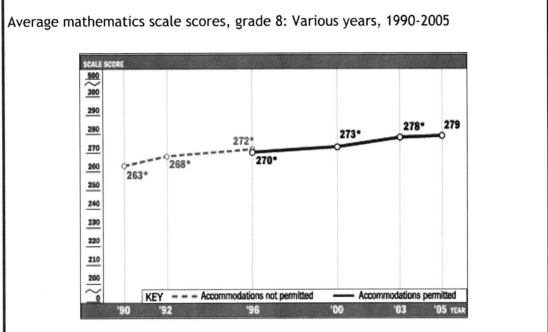

Average mathematics scale scores, grade 8: Various years, 1990-2005

<u>Significantly different</u> from 2005.
NOTE: The dashed and solid lines represent results based on administrations when <u>accommodations</u> were not permitted and when accommodations were permitted, respectively.

Source: Adapted from National Canter for Educational Statistics (NCES, 2005)

IMPACT OF ASSESSMENT ON TEACHING AND LEARNING

Data collected from assessment is used by teachers to plan and implement instruction that promotes student achievement at the conclusion of instructional objectives. Research refers to assessment-based instructional strategies as effective best practices.

FORMATIVE ASSESSMENT (Weber, E. 1999)
- Identifies immediate problems
- Provides data on individual learning objectives
- Demonstrates individual student progress
- Measures one set of experiences

SUMMATIVE ASSESSMENT (Weber, E. 1999)
- Measures learning over time
- Measures final results after longer period of time
- Provides data on learning objectives over time
- Often used to compare students' performances with other students' performances
- Often includes many units of study

Types of Standardized Test
- Diagnostic test
- Achievement test
- Aptitude test
- Norm Referenced test
- Criterion Referenced test

DIAGNOSTIC TEST – This screening test assesses young children's knowledge of fundamental skills that are predictive of future readiness for learning. Diagnostic assessment measures a student's current knowledge and skills for the purpose of identifying a suitable program of learning. It is the act or process of identifying or determining student's readiness, strength, or needs through evaluation of his or her history, observation, examination, or test in order to provide adequate instruction to meet the student's level of readiness to learn. Examples of diagnostic tests include the following:
- The Phonological Awareness Literacy Screening (PALS)
- The IQ Test

Achievement Test - An achievement test can be defined as a standardized test used to measure acquired learning. The following are examples of Achievement tests:

- The *Differential Ability Scales* (DAS) is a nationally normed and individually administered battery of cognitive and achievement tests. It is comprised of a cognitive battery subdivided into two overlapping levels of preschool level and school age levels and a school achievement test that measures the basic skills in word reading, spelling and arithmetic. The range of the DAS covers children from 2 years and 6 months to 17 years and 11 months. The DAS was developed from the *British Ability Scales* (BAS), by Collin D. Elliot and published by the Psychological Corporation in 1990.

Aptitude Test – This test measures a person's interest and ability and tests at what a person is really good. Examples of aptitude tests may include

- Talent Assessment test
- Career Aptitude test
- Job Aptitude test
- Intelligence Quotient (IQ) test

Norm Referenced Test (NRT) – This test compares student tests score or performance in one school district or state to those in the nation. A test is said to be norm-referenced when the translated score tells where a student ranks among a population of students who have taken the same tests (Cronbach, 1970). They are made to compare test takers to each other. On an NRT driving test, test-takers would be compared as to who knew the most or least about driving rules or who drove best or worst. Scores would be reported as a percentage rank with half scoring above and half below the mid-point (*Fair Test*). Examples of norm referenced tests include

- Stanford 9 Form TA which measures students performance in language, reading, and math
- Cognitive Abilities Test (CogAT) used to identify students for gifted programs

Criterion Referenced Tests (CRTs) – This test measures students' knowledge of the school curriculum taught. A test is said to be criterion-referenced when allowance is made for translating the test score into a statement about the behavior to be expected of the student with the score (Cronbach, 1970). Criterion-referenced tests (CRTs) are intended to measure how well a person has learned a specific body of knowledge and skills; in education, CRTs usually are made to determine if a student has learned the material taught in a specific grade or course. Examples of criterion referenced tests include the Virginia Standards of Learning (SOLs) given to grades 3-12 and the Multiple-choice tests that most people take to get a driver's license and on-the-road driving tests are both examples of criterion-referenced tests (Fair Test).

PORTFOLIO ASSESSMENT

Portfolio assessment is a collection of samples of students' work completed over the course of a semester or school year. Portfolios are meant to stimulate students' self-reflections by allowing them to review their strengths and weaknesses, and to let parent see how their child is growing and learning.

USING RUBRIC TO ASSESS PORTFOLIO

A rubric is often used as a criterion for assessing portfolio. A rubric is a scoring tool that lists the criteria for a piece of work or "what counts" with a point value that usually ranges from 1 to 4, with 4 being the highest. As a team, teachers and instructors can determine the criteria for their respective rubrics.

TEST TAKING STRATEGIES

In addition to learning the curricula contents, students should learn test-taking strategies. Teachers and instructors should not doubt the importance of teaching students how to take tests. When this author asked several students in both primary grades and college who always scored in the upper quartile (90 -100%) on tests to share their test-taking strategies, they offered the following helpful strategies for multiple choice tests. Students who employ these strategies, often score very high (90-100 percentile) on their tests. Students should always
- Think about what they are supposed to do.
- Read the test questions carefully.
- Look at the answer choices carefully.
- Mark the best answer and move on if they are absolutely sure.
- Look at the rest of the answer choices if they are not sure of the best answer.
- Eliminate answer choices they know definitely to be wrong.
- Try each answer choice in the blank for fill-in-the-blank type questions.
- Take their best guess when they are uncertain about the correct answer.
- Skip difficult items and return to them later.
- Make sure they mark the correct spaces on the answer document that align with the question they are answering.
- Answer all of the questions.

On the contrary, poor test takers (students who score 70 percentile and below) also shared their test-taking errors. They are very likely to
- Spend too much time on difficult items.
- Misread a question.

- Misread answer choices.
- Fill in the wrong answer space.
- Perform the wrong mathematics operations.
- Misread key words such as not, except, or opposite.
- Make a copying mistakes when rewriting a vertical math problem in a horizontal format and vice versa.
- Incorrectly transfer mathematic answers from the scratch papers to answer sheet.
- Read a passage prior to reading the question in a comprehension question.
- Perform the wrong mathematical operation.
- Fail to answer all the items.

Teachers and instructors should teach students the test-taking strategies in addition to teaching them the contents of the curriculum. The subsequent chart illustrates Brain Compatible Assessment tools available to teachers (Stephen, J., & Goldberg, D., 2001).

ASSESSMENT TOOLS AVAILABLE TO TEACHERS

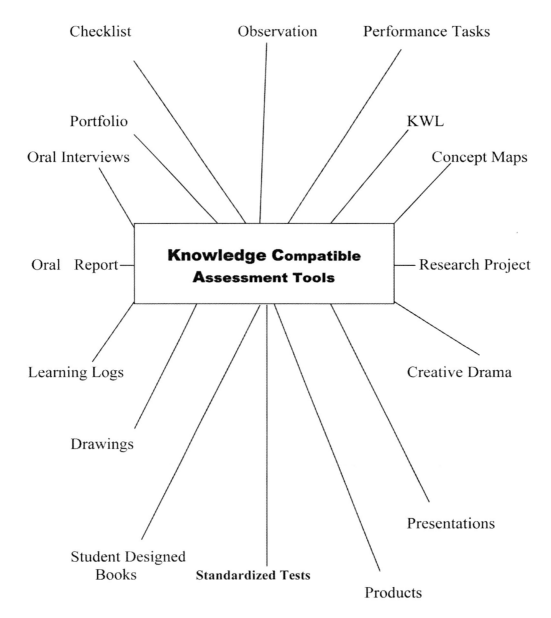

Adapted: Stevens, J., & Goldberg, D. (2001). *For the learners' sake: Brian-based instruction for the 21st century.* Tucson, AZ: Zephyr Press, p. 127.

The amount of time a teacher spends to teach procedures and routines at the beginning of the year will set the tone for classroom management, teaching and learning for the rest of the school year.
~ Dr. Ignatius Idio, 2006

CHAPTER 3
Classroom Management

Research studies tell us that in addition to other elements, two factors have significantly influenced student learning in our schools. These factors are teaching skills and classroom management. Research findings further point out that classrooms that experience more student misbehavior, also witness less time spent on task, and produce unproductive students. This chapter will define an effective classroom management, characteristics of effective classroom management, and classroom procedures that maximize active learning for all students. It will identify common challenging student behaviors and strategies for managing undesirable distractions.

EFFECTIVE CLASSROOM MANAGEMENT

Teachers are accountable for creating and maintaining a positive classroom community that is conducive to learning and conspicuously free of distracting discipline problems. They are responsible for creating a safe, secure, and positive classroom environment and for establishing positive relations between teachers and students and among students in the learning community. The following section will focus on the common characteristics of effective classroom environment.

Characteristics of Effective Classroom Management – Effective classroom management involves not only reacting to a problem but also preempting or preventing the occurrence of problems. Teachers who have clear goals, expectations, and visions for their students will include the following characteristics in their classroom management strategies:
- Teachers model clear expectations, structure, and consistency.
- Teachers engage students in instruction that is responsive to student needs (e.g., curricula are aligned, matched, or differentiated to suit all students learning needs).
- Teachers employ direct instruction of expectations and reinforcement of desired behaviors (e.g., modeling, guided practice, shaping of successive approximations, and interesting opportunities for independent practice).

- Teachers integrate effective use of procedures (i.e., daily routines and procedures that are clearly stated and posted in the class for all students to see).
- Teachers serve as a coach or facilitator, guiding students to the desired goal.
- Students actively participate in their learning.
- Students are involved, beginning on the first day, in the decision making of the course of their study.
- Students vigorously research, discuss, create projects, and use technology to make discoveries based on their choices.
- Students are active participants in the learning process.
- Students participate in "real-life" activities through collaboration, exploration, and discovery with peers.
- Instruction and learning are assessed regularly.
- Student and teacher behaviors are managed to achieve instructional goal and objectives.
- Students are motivated to maximize their learning potentials.
- Students respect one another and their teachers.
- Teachers establish procedures for assigning and collecting homework or "lifework."
- Teachers walk around the room to attend to students' needs.
- Teachers organize students in groups such as Monday, Tuesday, Wednesday, Thursday, and Friday to enhance transition activities.
- Teachers talk directly to students by calling their names to show respect to students.
- Teachers use the "I Statement" (e.g., When you talk so loudly, I become distracted, and I have difficulty attending to other students in the classroom).
- Teachers address students with courtesy to be positive role models.

CLASSROOM PROCEDURES AND ROUTINES
Specific routines may include the following specific activities:
- Reciting the Pledge of Allegiance
- Taking daily attendance
- Displaying class rules, rewards, and consequences
- Posting restroom and water breaks schedule in the classroom
- Writing homework agenda on the board
- Insisting that students write homework in their agendas
- Establishing clear procedure for completing and turning in homework assignments
- Providing instructions for completing center activities
- Posting lunch menu in the classroom
- Displaying schedule for enrichment or special classes

Source: (Adapted from Dr. France Boutin & Dr. Chris Chinien: "Characteristics of effective classroom management")

Specific Incidents Related to Classroom Management

- Failure to perform tasks
- Disturbing classroom activities
- Failure to pay attention
- Failure to abide by rules or follow directions
- Tardiness
- Failure to follow instructions
- Procrastination
- Lack of organizational skills
- Failure to complete and turn in class and homework assignments
- Frequently getting out of seat
- Excessive talking

COMMUNICATING STUDENT PROGRESS TO PARENTS

Effective classroom management includes talking and listening to students, teacher-parent partnership, and a variety of ways to communicate student progress to parents. Teachers should communicate to students by teaching the procedures, routines, and expectations from the very first day of the school year. They should listen to students actively and empathetically, by paraphrasing and reflecting to make the students feel validated. The goal of active listening is to elicit and foster greater involvement of the students in the dialogues. The following methods of communicating with parents have been proven effective

- Sending home student weekly progress folder (e.g., Friday folder sent home every Friday with student's papers and parent's comment and signature form. The folder must be returned by the following Monday after parent has reviewed it and sign the signature form.)
- Sending home interim report on student progress; this is usually sent home in the middle of each quarter to make parents aware of student's midterm achievement. (This is particularly important with low performing student whose parent might want to schedule a conference with the teacher to discuss academic needs and progress.)
- Sending home quarterly or semester report cards
- Telephoning parent to report on student progress

- E-mailing parent to communicate student progress. It is a very fast mode of communication. Early in the school year, preferably at Back-to-School night, collect e-mail addresses from parents who have access to Internet and store them in address book solely for communicating with parents. Parent's confidentiality must be kept
- Sending notes to parent to highlight students achievement and conduct
- Scheduling parent-teacher conference regularly to meet with parent to discuss student progress
- Organizing events at school and invite parents to participate (Such events may include: Back-to-School night, Math & Science Night, Social Science & History Night, Honor Roll Award Ceremony, Concerts and other extra-curricular activities on campus.)
- Maintaining cordial, friendly, and welcoming attitudes that are inviting to parents
- Encouraging parent volunteerism (Some schools like, Pennington Traditional School in Manassas, Virginia require all parents to volunteer 10 hours of the school year per child. If a parent has two children, the parent volunteers 20 hours per year, and the parent signs a contract to fulfill the volunteer hours after the student is admitted into Pennington School.)
- Protecting students' and parents' confidentialities

Source: (Adapted from Dr. France Boutin & Dr. Chris Chinien, "Characteristic of effective classroom management")

TRIGGER OF STUDENT MISBEHAVIOR

Research studies have identified some common factors that trigger student misbehavior. These triggers include environmental factors, external factors, internal factors, and other people.

- Environmental factors – These are things that happen around a student to trigger distracting behavior, such as transitioning from a familiar environment to a new and different one or transferring to a new school.
- External factors – These may include something a student does that is distracting to himself or herself, such as frequently getting out of seat.
- Internal distraction – These are things a student does to exhibit unacceptable behavior, such as high level of anxiety or stress.
- Other people – What other people do may trigger student misbehavior in the classroom. For example, other students may avoid or isolate one student from social interaction, which may cause social withdrawal.

PURPOSE OF MISBEHAVIOR

Misbehavior of any kind is purposeful. When a student misbehaves, teachers should evaluate the behavior to determine why the student is acting that way. Research studies have identified the following as the purposes for behaviors of concern or misbehavior among students:

- Attention – Students misbehave to get attention. For example, a student might know ahead of time what button to push to set in motion an adult's feelings and reactions. Usually, teachers feel annoyed when student exhibits behaviors of concern and react by reminding and coaxing. Students will respond by stopping the behavior temporarily only to resume the same behavior or distract in a different way.
- Power – Sometimes, students display behaviors of concern to challenge the authority figure or teacher in the classroom. They feel in control, but the teacher feels angry or provoked and may even fight the students. The teacher may also argue or give in. The students respond by becoming aggressive or temporarily submit with "defiant compliance."
- Revenge – Students misbehave with intent to hurt others to revenge their anger. The teacher feels hurt but does not want to overlook the incident. He or she wants to get even. Students desire further revenge by heightening the hurtful behavior of concern; the more the teacher complains, the more students feel validated in displaying behaviors of concern.

- Display of inadequacy – Students exhibit behaviors of concern because they expect nothing positive from other people. The teacher feels despair and develops a sense of hopelessness to the extent of throwing in the towel. His or her reaction includes agreeing with students that nothing can be done.

Teachers should develop "replacement behaviors" to manage behaviors of concern. For example, students must raise their hands to get the teacher's attention. A teacher must actually teach expected, achievable, behaviors necessary to enhance the students' abilities to learn and participate adequately.

MANAGING STUDENT MISBEHAVIOR

Teachers should take proactive intervention to prevent misbehavior from escalating to a crisis stage. The plan is to regain focus or to bring the students back to equilibrium or back on task. When students are off task, out of their seats, talking out of turn, the appropriate intervention should include changing the nature of the task. The teacher may involve students in activities that engage their interest by providing meaningful options or choices for the students.

When a student uses provocative or threatening language, teachers should focus on removing all triggers that prompted the displayed misbehavior and should employ the school's crisis prevention procedure (all school must have a crisis prevention procedure) and disengage himself from the student and get help immediately. It is important for the teacher to note that there is the likelihood for escalation to run its course.

When a student becomes physically aggressive, displays property destruction, begins to inflict self-injuries, or becomes violent towards other students, the teacher should use the school's crisis intervention plan whereby the unruly student is removed from the classroom environment until de-escalation is attained.

When the student is undergoing de-escalation, teachers should be aware of several overt signals. For example, student may show social withdrawal, be in denial, blame others and attempt to justify or minimize the problem.

For intervention, teachers should not nag, blame, or force an apology. Instead, it is appropriate to introduce interesting activity that is familiar and less stressful to the student in order to minimize any chance of frustration or failure for the student.

BRINGING STUDENT BACK TO EQUILIBRIUM

The primary goal of behavior management is to bring the student with misbehavior problems back to normalcy or equilibrium. In other words, teachers employ interventions that will reengage the student in academic focus. The recovery period starts when a misbehaved student attempts to correct the problem. Teachers should proceed with the following intervention:

- Allow student to regain equilibrium and reestablish routines
- Provide stabilizing activity, safe environment for recovery
- Calmly follow through with consequences for problem behavior
- Positively reinforce any displays of appropriate behavior
- Provide opportunity for changing factors and preventing re-escalation
- Provide opportunity for self-awareness

Source: Adapted from work of George Sugai: *Positive Behavior Intervention Support (PBIS).* A handout from Carolyn Lamm, ITS, at a workshop on "Challenging Behaviors/ Classroom management" PWCS, March 8 & 14, 2006.

REWARDS THAT PROMOTE TIME ON TASK

The author of this book has used research-based strategies and tips acquired from years of professional training programs, on-the-job experiences, observations of colleague teachers in their classrooms, and the use of human relations skills with students in grades 4 -6. He can therefore, assert with conviction that these strategies and tips do promote in students time on task, the desire to meet and exceed behavior expectation, and overall increased academic success among students. It is important to note also that the author's success depended on his teaching style and professional growth. Therefore, he feels compelled to share these rewards, strategies, and tips with current and potential teachers, especially beginning teachers (with less than five years of teaching experience). When a student behaves or meets classroom expectations, teachers should seize the moment to reward the student in order to sustain the behavior with the hope that it will become contagious.

- Treasure box pass – When a student turns in homework (lifework as it is called here at Pennington Traditional School), completes assigned class work, or follows rules, this author will reward him/her with one treasure pass for that day. On Friday, the student can trade in the pass for items from the box (parents and teacher donate goodies for the treasure box).
- Post it "Thank you note" – The note simply says "Thank you (student's name) for making my day yesterday. I hope you do so again today!" Post the note on the student's desk each morning before he/she arrives. On Friday, the students who received a Thank you note win a special treat.
- Win extra recess for our class – When all students walk quietly in line to and from special and enrichment classes, the whole class earns 5 to 10 minutes of recess. Teachers will be amazed at how much an extra 5 minutes of recess mean to students. The extra recess is usually taken on Fridays, added to the regular recess time.
- Excellent stamp – Students who had an exemplary week will have their Friday folders (weekly progress folders) stamped with "EXCELLENT."
- "PERK" – An acrostic for
  - o Positive
  - o Enrichment
  - o Rewards for
  - o Kids

When a student behaves exemplary for a given day, the teacher awards one PERK for that day. On Friday, the student can trade the PERK for a special treat or privilege.

CONSEQUENCES THAT SUPPORT LEARNING

When student does not follow the class or school rules, this author employs both the school-wide and/or classroom consequences to redirect student behavior. For example, when a student runs rather than walks in the hall way, throws food at another student in the cafeteria, uses playground equipment in an unsafe manner, teases another student, disrespects another student or adult in the building, teachers can use the color card system, which stipulates the consequences for such violations. The color cards are green, yellow, and red. Each color designates the frequency of misbehavior and corresponding level of consequence. The system works in the following manner:

- Green card – For example, when a student runs in the hallway, any teacher in the building will stop the student and talk to him or her. The teacher may walk the student back to class or send a note with the student to the homeroom teacher explaining what the student did to deserve a green card or warning. If a student is off task or gets out of his or her seat frequently, the teacher gives a green card for warning.

- Yellow card – If a student earns a green card and repeats the same violation, a yellow card is given to raise the level of consequence from a warning to the taking away privileges. For example, a student with a yellow card may lose 5 minutes of recess.

- Red card – If a student repeatedly commits the same or similar infraction or distraction, a red card is issued. Depending on the severity of the infraction or distraction, the student is referred to the assistant principal or counselor or a note is sent home to the parents. The teacher may follow-up with a telephone call or e-mail to the parent for possible conference to discuss what to do to redirect the student back to the acceptable behavior or equilibrium.

The success or failure of the above reward or consequence strategies will depend on two things. First, teachers must teach the reward and consequence process to each group of students at the beginning of the school year. They must make sure that students practice the procedures needed to master and become vested in the program. Teachers must be consistent when implementing each of the strategies. If done otherwise, they are bound to be less than effective and can lead to increased misbehavior among students. It is often advisable to discuss your discipline plan or behavior management system with your administrators or supervisors before implementing it because their support is crucial for the success of the plan or system. The next section contains samples of group activities that approximate actual student behavior. Pre-service teachers or interns can work in groups or individually to brainstorm solutions to the problem.

GROUP ACTIVITY #1

Problem #1: Failure to abide by rules

Background – In a music class, a student decides to put her equipment away five minutes before regular dismissal. The rest of the class continued with the activity. She sat and did not participate for the last five minutes of class. This was the last period before lunch (Adapted from lovetoteach, online 1/29/06).

Directions – Read and analyze that incident carefully and indicate what exactly you would do to address the problem. Record your group's responses and be ready to share the responses with the rest of the class.

GROUP ACTIVITY #2

Problem #2: A difficult parent

Background – You have a parent in your classroom who is extremely upset over little things. You were out sick on Monday and Tuesday. This parent chewed your substitute teacher out because his son (almost 10 years old) got his new sweat shoes all muddy while playing kickball at recess. When this parent came to pick up his son at the end of the day and while walking toward the car, he noticed the muddy shoes. He came right back and shouted rudely at the substitute in front of other parents and children.

You can understand why this parent was upset about the shoes. However, you feel his outburst is inappropriate to say the least. This same parent was angry with you last month when his son was sick and you sent him to the school nurse. The parent was called. He was so furious because he was called from work. Mom does not work, so it isn't like he was losing a day's pay. You have a meeting with this parent on Friday afternoon. (Adapted from lovetoteach, online 1/29/06).

Directions – Read and analyze that incident carefully and indicate what exactly you would do to address the problem. Record your group's responses and be ready to share them with the rest of the class.

Problem #3: Failure to perform task

Background – Children in this third grade class were asked to do activities in their activity packets before going to the stations of their choice. Some students were not doing all their pocket activities (Adapted from lovetoteach, online 1/29/06).

Directions – Read and analyze that incident carefully and indicate exactly what you would do to address the problem. Record your group's responses and be ready to share them with the rest of the class.

Problem #4: Violent behavior

Background – Your 5th graders have just returned from physical education (PE). This was the last period before lunch. You noticed that as the students walked back to their seats, one student, nicknamed J. T. said to another student: *"I hate you, you SOB."* As he approached his seat, J. T. also kicked his chair violently. The students were very frightened. J.T. is known to have tempers and likes to call the other students names. He likes to use vulgar language. His 3rd and 4th grade teachers have had issues with his use of the F-word on other students in the cafeteria and in art class. The school counselor indicated that J. T. has been referred several times by his 3rd and 4th grade teachers for using vulgar language. The Parents have met at conferences to address his violent behaviors and use of vulgarity.

Directions – Read and analyze that incident carefully and indicate what exactly you would do to address the problem. Record your group's responses and be ready to share them with the rest of the class.

"Every Child Deserves Our Best."
– (NCAE & NEA, 2005)

CHAPTER 4
What Some States are Doing to Narrow the Achievement Gap

How State Policymakers Can Help

K. Haycock (2002) offers a few suggestions on how state policymakers can begin to focus on the "academic core" by

- Breaking myths and changing expectations means creating "clear and unequivocal" standards, assessments, and accountability systems (p. 12). Reports should document progress by groups and include information on all schools in the state.

- Increasing the quality of teaching means more than hiring more and better teachers. Teachers also need to be distributed more equitably. New York forbids using uncertified teachers in low-performing schools, while Louisiana issues a "report card" that compares teacher quality in the district as a whole with the district's poorest school.

- Upgrading curricula means making the content and not just the number of classes a requirement for graduation. Texas, for example, has moved to make the college prep curriculum the default curriculum.

- Helping low-performing students and teachers means providing more money for instruction, professional development, and assessment. Helping low-performing students and teachers may also mean providing more flexibility in instructional time.

- Creating equity in resources means redirecting state funds to poorer schools; forty-two (42) states give more money to the wealthiest schools than the poorest schools. New York has the greatest inequity, spending $1.17 million less per elementary school in the poorest districts. According to Haycock, money alone won't help, but some of the things that money can buy will. Several states have commenced a range of strategies to narrow the achievement gap. For example: Missouri State has set up a state task force on K-12 issues and released a report in 2002 that concluded that improving teacher quality is the single most important factor in eliminating the achievement gap. The report recommends raising teacher quality through increased accountability, better understanding of urban issues, and financial incentives for teachers in low-performing schools.

The following states are doing some creative things to narrow the achievement gap:

- **North Carolina:** Governor Michael Easley has appointed an Education First task force to examine best instructional practices from higher-performing schools in order to learn how to close the achievement gap. The goal of the school leaders is to eliminate the achievement gap by 2010.

- **Texas:** The state's accountability system mandates schools each year to show a minimum proficiency level (percent proficiency) in each student subgroup. In the five years since this legislation was enacted, the percentage of African-American students passing the statewide exams rose by 31%, and the percentage of Hispanic students passing the exam rose by 29%. Meanwhile, the percentage of the white students passing the exam grew by only 18%. These figures mean that the achievement gap in Texas closed by 13% and 11% for African American and Hispanic students respectively.

- **Indiana Department of Education:** This school district's accountability system holds schools responsible for educating Indiana students based on high standards and challenges them to improve achievement continuously. Beginning with data from the 2002 ISTEP tests, the Department of Education will determine if Indiana school corporations and public schools have met Adequate Yearly Progress goals under the federal No Child Left Behind Act of 2002 (NCLB). Beginning in the school year 2005-2006, the Indiana State Board of Education shall annually place all public schools and those non-public schools that voluntarily seek accreditation in a school improvement and performance category based on results from assessments in English and mathematics. Adequate Yearly Progress under NCLB will be a criteria for category placement" (Indiana Department of Education, webmaster@doe.state.in.us)

- **Nevada Department of Education:** This school district has "developed a research-based school improvement process – Student Achievement Gap Elimination (SAGE) – to assist school and district improvement efforts. As a school goes through this process, it carries out the following steps: (a) a comprehensive needs assessment, (b) an inquiry process, (c) a master plan design, and (d) implementation and evaluation" (Dr. Keith W. Rheault, Nevada Dept. of Edu).

- **Georgia Department of Education:** On July 1, 2003 the Georgia Department of Education (GDOE) created the School Improvement

Division in the Office of Teacher and Student Support. The goal is to design and implement a coherent and sustained statewide system of support and process for improvement, providing local education agencies (local school systems, herein referred to as LEAs) and schools in Georgia with tools and resources as well as intensive support for schools not making Adequate Yearly Progress (AYP).

- The School Improvement Division will work collaboratively with Georgia's Regional Education Service Agencies (RESAs) to support LEAs with schools not making AYP. Four Regional Support Teams, including School Improvement, Title I and Curriculum and Instruction GDOE personnel, RESA School Improvement Specialists, Professional Standards Commission Title IIA Regional Staff, GLRS Regional Representatives, Education Technology Training Center Regional Representatives, and College and University Representatives have been formed to provide regional support and improvement process training across the state.

- The School Improvement Division has prioritized statewide support by analyzing school performance and reform efforts. Schools in Needs Improvement Years 2-7 and priority Needs Improvement Year 1 schools will receive the support of a GDOE Leadership Facilitator (on-site coach). The School Improvement Division and RESAs will identify Regional Support Team members and distinguished K-12 educators to serve all schools having made AYP only one year and who need targeted assistance to make Adequate Yearly Progress another year to be removed from Needs Improvement status.

- The School Improvement Division will offer the following Continuum of Services to LEAs/schools in Georgia:
  A. **Analysis and Planning**: Provide tools for collecting and analyzing qualitative and quantitative data, guidance for analyzing causes and establishing improvement priorities, and a model for action planning and matching needs to resources.
  B. **Collaborative Implementation**: Develop an online resource guide of research-based programs and strategies, serve as a broker of programs and interventions to facilitate goal attainment, and provide technical assistance with implementation.
  C. **Professional Learning**: Coordinate programs to build LEA/schools capacity, broker services to facilitate training and development, and guide implementation of national professional development standards.
  D. **Quality Assurance**: Disaggregate/analyze outcomes & policies, report impact on student achievement, provide guidelines for program evaluation, & recommend action.

E. **Leader Quality**: Provide focused leadership training and development to support the Georgia Performance Standards implementation, provide guidance and ongoing support for GDOE Leadership Facilitators, and coordinate the systematic use of SREB Leadership Modules targeting standards-based education and research-based school improvement priorities.

- The School Improvement Division will utilize web and print media to publish high quality tools and resources including the School Improvement Fieldbook: A Guide to Advancing Student Achievement in Georgia Schools and the Georgia Standards for School Performance and Performance Review Instrument (GDOE --Closing the Student Achievement Gap).

Proof of Progress

In spite of the persistent challenges, many states have shown that the achievement gap is not insurmountable. For example, the Education Trust reports that in

- Texas: "The NAEP writing scores for eighth-grade African Americans are equal to or higher than writing scores of white students in seven states."
- Virginia: "This state boasts one of the nation's smallest achievement gaps between whites and Hispanics. Here, eighth-grade Hispanic students had the highest NAEP writing scores for Hispanic students in any states."
- Department of Defense (DoD) schools: In spite of "high mobility, minority students in DoD schools do better on NAEP than their counterparts, yielding a smaller achievement gap. Fourth-grade white students in DoD schools outscored their African-American counterparts by an average of 17 points on the NAEP reading tests – a considerably smaller gap than the national average of 32 points."

Source: (Adapted from *Closing the Achievement gap.* NGA Center for Best Practices, Washington, D.C. Retrieved on 4/9/06).

WHAT SOME SCHOOLS ARE DOING TO
NARROW THE ACHIEVEMENT GAP

According to research, what schools do matters. K. Haycock (2002) focused on the following changes in the educational systems that have proven helpful in closing the racial and economic achievement gaps. School should

- **Have uniform standards**. High-poverty schools often set shockingly low standards for their students. Haycock says, "Clear and public standards for what children should learn at benchmark grade levels are a critical part of solving this problem" (p. 9). The progress of Kentucky, the first state to adopt such standards-based reform, is "clear and compelling" (p. 10).

- **Make the curriculum challenging**. Uniform standards mean nothing without a rigorous curriculum. Haycock says that high school students who take college-preparatory courses perform much better on standardized tests than students who take vocational classes, even if these students were not high performers to begin with. In 1992, just under 26% of African American and 23% of Latino 10th-graders were on college prep track, compared to 34% of whites. Rigorous course work is also "the single most important determinant of who succeeds in college" (p. 10).

- **Help students catch up**. Higher standards will only frustrate students who lack a good foundation in reading and mathematics. Haycock writes "We need to double or even triple the amount (and quality) of instruction that they get" (p. 11). Kentucky gives high-poverty schools more money to extend instruction, while San Diego devotes more of the school day to literacy and mathematics for low-performing students.

- **Provide good teachers**. Poor and minority students are more likely than their affluent and majority counterparts to be taught by underqualified teachers (no matter how qualification is measured). Further research shows that good teaching is "the thing that unquestionably matters most" (Haycock, 2004, p. 12) to student learning. Studies of schools in Texas and Tennessee also show that teaching matters regardless of race, class, or prior achievement. For example, a study by Harvard economist Ronald found that Texas students in low-performing schools that hired the best teachers eventually outperformed students from high-performing schools that hired from the bottom of the teaching pool.

In response to NCLB mandates, several school districts have instituted a range of strategies to narrow the achievement gap. Douglas Reeves and his colleagues from the Center for Performance Assessment (as quoted in Robert Rothman, 2001/02) found that schools that have plans to close achievement gap share many common characteristics, including

- a focus on academic achievement;
- clear curriculum choices, specifically, an emphasis on reading, writing, and mathematics;
- frequent assessment of student progress with multiple opportunities for improvement;
- written responses in performance assessments;
- external scoring of assessments.

Examples of schools that have in place successful programs to close achievement gaps include the following systems:

- **El Paso, Texas, Schools**. K. Haycock (2002) wrote that El Paso, Texas, is an example of a school district that has worked hard to close the achievement gap. Local education leaders set high standards for students and provided more training and support for teachers. According to Haycock, the results are "no more low-performing schools and increased achievement for all groups of students, with bigger increases among the groups that have historically been behind" (p. 12).

- **Department of Defense (DoD) schools**. According to the 1998 NAEP survey, 85 percent of black students and 93 percent of Hispanic students in DoD's domestic schools rated teacher expectations for their performance "very positive," compared to 52 percent of black students and 53 percent of Hispanic students nationwide.

- **Lanier Middle School in Houston**. This school tried a number of strategies to improve instruction in mathematics and reading. For example, in mathematics, the school provided additional instruction for the seventh graders who needed "another shot" of the subject and added a second teacher for eighth graders who needed remediation. In English language arts, the school implemented new instructional strategies to develop students' abilities to articulate the meaning of what they read and to build their reading stamina. Lanier also created after-school reading and writing groups for Latino students. As a result of these efforts, the performance of the targeted students increased dramatically, and the achievement gaps at Lanier have narrowed substantially. In 2000-2001, 89% of African American students and 86% of Hispanic students passed the state tests, and the school's rating moved up a notch, to recognized. As a result of its efforts, Lanier also became a Beacon school, eligible for a development grant from the Houston Annenberg Challenge.

- **Houston schools**. These schools are required by state law to report the performance of racial and ethnic groups. In fact, under the state's accountability system, schools can be rated successful only if all groups

- white, African American, Hispanic, and economically disadvantaged students - meet state standards.

The researchers have found examples of similarly successful schools in other districts as well, including Riverside and Orange counties in California. However, the researchers note that most of the schools they have studied are elementary schools, mainly because high schools may not be able to implement the instructional changes the elementary schools have put in place. "There is less control over the curriculum at the high school level," K. Haycock points out.

Source: Rothman, R. (2001/02). *The Journal of the Annenburg Challenge.* Vol 5, No. 2. At: http://www.annenberginstitute.org/challenge/pubs/cj/gap_cj.htm#approaches (11 April 06)

> *"It takes a whole nation to eliminate the achievement gap in our schools."*
> *— (Ignatius E. Idio, 2006)*

CHAPTER 5
A Summary of Research Findings About What Works in Teaching and Learning

In the 1960s, conventional wisdom about education maintained that minority and disadvantaged students from impoverished communities and districts performed poorly in schools solely because of the "inequitable distribution of educational resources" (Bennett, et al., 1986). In response to that conventional awareness of student academic achievement inequity, the U.S. Congress commissioned an extensive national survey that became known as the *Coleman Report*. The conclusion of the Coleman educational research stated that "unequal achievement could not be ascribed to unequal school resources."

That report so gravely offended the conventional wisdom of the era that the subsequent years of educational research have been inundated by a quest to contradict the conclusion of the Coleman Report. Of course, educators are still wrestling with the same issue today in the twenty first century. The only certainty about the disparity in achievement gap is that the problem has become more complex and deeper and the desire to eradicate it has grown more intense. The good news is that between 1960s and 2000s the achievement gap between the minority and disadvantaged students and their majority and more affluent counterparts has narrowed somewhat. The fundamental question that continues to preoccupy policymakers is will the achievement gap ever be eliminated?

The following research findings on what works to improve student achievement have been summarized from the perspective of homes, classrooms, and schools in chapter 5 of this book.

HOME PERSPECTIVES
- **Curriculum of the Home**. Parents are their children's first and most influential teachers. What they do to help their children learn is more significant to academic success than how well-off the family is.
- **Reading to Children**. The best way for parents to help their children become better readers is to read to them, even when they are young.

Children benefit most from reading aloud when they discuss stories, learn to identify letters and words, and talk about the meaning of words.

- **Counting**. A good way to teach children simple arithmetic is to build on their informal knowledge. This is why learning to count everyday objects is an effective basis for early arithmetic lesson.
- **Developing Talent**. Many highly successful individuals have above-average but not extraordinary intelligence. Accomplishment in a particular activity is often more dependent upon hard work and self-discipline than on innate ability.
- **Ideals**. Belief in the value of hard work, the importance of personal responsibility, and the importance of education itself contributes to greater success in school.

CLASSROOM PERSPECTIVES

- **Getting Parents Involved**. Parental involvement helps children learn more effectively. Teachers who are successful at involving parents in their children's schoolwork are successful because they work at it.
- **Phonics**. Children get a better start in reading if they are taught phonics. Learning phonics helps them to understand the relationship between letters and sounds and to 'break the code' that links the words they hear with the words they see in print.
- **Reading Comprehension**. Children get more out of a reading assignment when the teacher precedes the lesson with background information and follows it with discussion.
- **Science Experiments**. Children learn science best when they are able to do experiments so they can witness science in action.
- **Storytelling**. Telling young children stories can motivate them to read. Storytelling also introduces them to cultural values and literary traditions before they can read, write, and talk about stories by themselves.
- **Teaching Writing**. The most effective way to teach writing is to teach it as a process of brainstorming, composing, revising, and editing.
- **Learning Mathematics**. Children in early grades learn mathematics more effectively when they use physical objects in their lesson.
- **Estimating**. Although students need to learn how to find exact answers to arithmetic problems, good math students also learn the helpful skill of estimating answers. This skill can be taught.
- **Student Ability and Effort**. Children's understanding of the relationship between being smart and hard work changes as they grow.
- **Managing Classroom Time**. How much time students are actively engaged in learning contributes strongly to their achievement. The amount of time

available for learning is determined by the instructional and management skills of the teacher and the priorities set by the school administration.

- **Direct Instruction**. When teachers explain exactly what the students are expected to learn, and demonstrate the steps needed to accomplish a particular academic task, students learn more.
- **Tutoring**. Students tutoring other students can lead to improved academic achievement for both student and tutor, and to positive attitudes toward coursework.
- **Memorization**. Memorizing can help students absorb and retain the factual information on which understanding and critical thought are based.
- **Questioning**. Student achievement rises when teachers ask questions that require students to apply, analyze, synthesize, and evaluate information in addition to recalling facts.
- **Study Skills**. The ways in which children study influence strongly how much they learn. Teachers can often help children develop better study skills.
- **Homework or Lifework Quantity**. Student achievement rises significantly when teachers regularly assign homework or lifework and students consciously do it.
- **Homework or Lifework Quality**. Well-designed homework or lifework assignments relate directly to class work and extend students' learning beyond the classroom. Homework/lifework is most useful when teachers carefully prepare the assignment, thoroughly explain it, and give prompt comments and criticisms when the work is completed.
- **Assessment**. Frequent and systematic monitoring of students' progress helps students, parents, teachers, administrators, and policymakers identify strengths and weaknesses in learning and instruction.

SCHOOL PERSPECTIVES

- **Effective Schools**. The most important characteristics of effective schools are strong instructional leadership, safe and orderly climate, school-wide emphasis on basic skills, high teacher expectations for pupil progress.
- **School Climate**. Schools that encourage academic achievement focus on the importance of scholastic success and maintaining order and discipline.
- **Discipline.** Schools contribute to their students' academic achievement by establishing, communicating, and enforcing fair and constant discipline policies.
- **Unexcused Absences**. Unexcused absences decrease when parents are promptly informed that their children are not attending school.
- **Teacher Supervision**. Teachers welcome professional suggestions about improving their work, but they rarely receive them. Principals who are

good supervisors make themselves available to help teachers. They make teachers feel they can come for help without being branded failures. When supervisors comment constructively on teachers' specific skills, they help teachers become more effective and improve teachers' morale.

- **Cultural Literacy**. Students read more fluently and with greater understanding if they have background knowledge of the past and present. Such knowledge and understanding is called cultural literacy.

- **History**. Skimpy requirements and declining enrollment in history class are contributing to a decline in students' knowledge of the past.

- **Foreign Language**. The best way to learn a foreign language in school is to start early and to study it intensively over many years.

- **Rigorous Courses**. The stronger the emphasis on academic course, the more advanced the subject matter, and the more rigorous the textbooks, the more high school students learn. Subjects that are learned mainly in school rather than at home, such as science and math, are most influenced by the number and kind of courses taken.

- **Acceleration**. Advancing gifted students at a faster pace results in their achieving more than similarly gifted students who are taught at a normal rate.

- **Extracurricular Activities**. High school students who complement their academic studies with extracurricular activities gain experience that contributes to their success in college.

- **Preparation for Work**. Business leaders report that students with solid basic skills and positive work attitudes are more likely to find and keep jobs than students with vocational skills alone.

Eradicating the achievement gap between the disadvantaged and minority students and their majority and more well-to-do counterparts in our nation's schools should be the fundamental desire of every citizen and organization including parents, tax payers, teachers, school districts, states, and federal governments because collectively we are stakeholders in our children's education now and for generations yet to come.

PART TWO

From A *S.M.A.R.T* Goal to Effective Lesson Plan
Philip Michael Pennington School
Team or Individual Goals
4th Grade Teacher - 2005-2006

Goal Statement #1 (TEAM GOAL based upon a review of the data and assessments for their grade level)

Team Goal
Ninety-five percent of the fourth grade students at Pennington School will receive a score of either *consistent* or *reasonable* on the fourth grade Writing Predictor test by June 2006 through the use of Writers Workshop, writing prompts, thinking maps, critical thinking activities, and curriculum management systems or CMS tests.

Specific Strategies: Teachers will implement the curriculum at Pennington School under the guidance of the principal and language arts advisor. The CMS unit tests will be given throughout the year.

Measurable: 95% of the fourth grade students at Pennington School will receive a score of either *consistent* or *reasonable* on the fourth grade Writing Predictor test by June 2006.

Attainable: Focus will be on the writing process, critical thinking, and thinking maps.

Results: In order to reach the performance target of 95% of Pennington School fourth grade students receiving a score of either *consistent* or *reasonable* on the fourth grade Writing Predictor test, teachers will implement the following strategies:
    * Thinking Maps
    * Writers Workshop

* Note taking
* Class writing prompts
* Critical thinking activities
* CMS tests

Time Bound: By June 2006

IDEA CHART

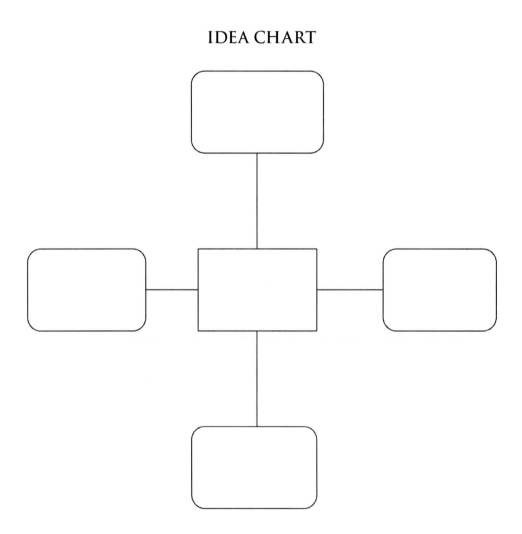

SEQUENCE CHART

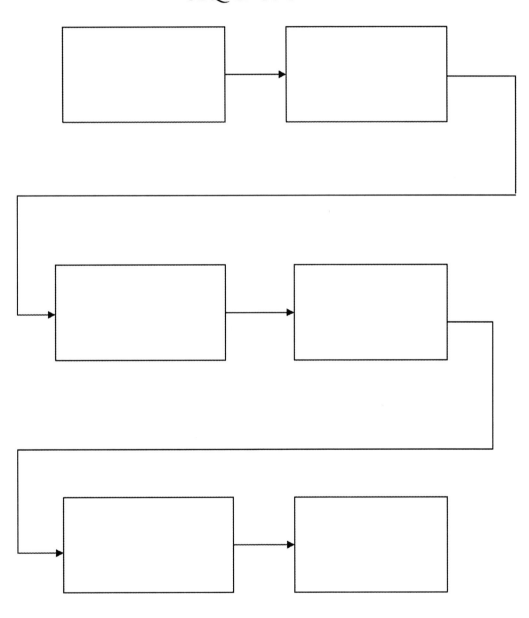

BRAINSTORMING CHART

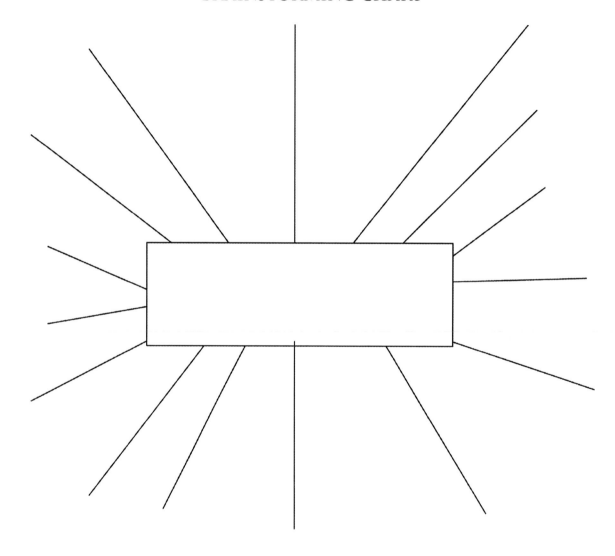

BLOOM'S TAXONOMY:
HIGHER-LEVEL QUESTIONS

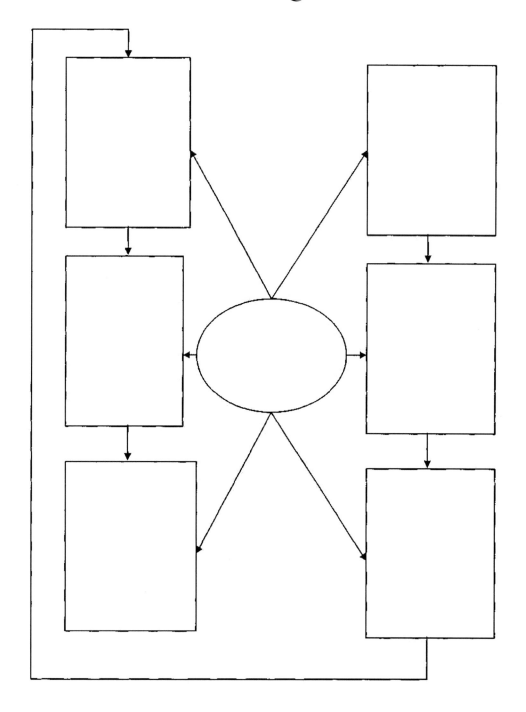

MAIN IDEA & DETAILS CHART

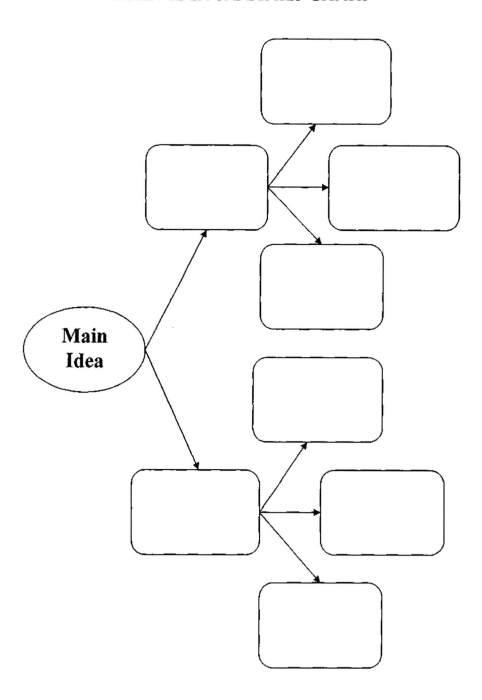

CHARACTER WEB

What Am I?

How the character Looks	How the character acts
1. _____	1. _____
2. _____	2. _____
3. _____	3. _____
4. _____	4. _____

Character's name

_____

How the character feels	What the character says
1. _____	1. _____
2. _____	2. _____
3. _____	3. _____
4. _____	4. _____

GLOSSARY

Accountability – policies developed to hold schools and school systems responsible for the academic results of their students

Achievement Gap – the difference in school achievement among different groups (and subgroups) of students such as racial/ethnic groups, income level, etc

Andragogy - the art of helping adults learn; relating to adult learning

Assessment – measuring student performance or collecting data and making judgments; This term is often used synonymously with testing

AYP/Adequate Yearly Progress – a signaling system to tell whether schools are on- track to teach all students what they need to know in each school year

Compacting – modifying

Content Standards – statements of what students from Kindergarten through 12th grade should know and be able to do in the core content areas; For example: English/Language Arts, Mathematics, Science, and Social Studies

Curriculum – the subject material that teachers cover with students in class; It is often referred to what subject matters that students should learn and be able to do

Data – facts or figures from which conclusions can be made; information

Differentiation of Instruction – a teacher's response to learner's needs guided by general principles of differentiation of instruction using a range of instructional and management strategies; leveling the playing field for all students

Disaggregate – to break down information/data by different groups, either by race, ethnicity, income levels, gender, etc

Equilibrium – bringing back to normal or on task

Evaluation – making judgment about measurements

Exigency – urgency, demand, constraint, or requirement

Formative Assessment – a formative assessment is an assessment generally carried out throughout a course or project

Intelligence Quotient Test – a test originally calculated using the <u>ratio</u> of a person's mental age (as measured by a standardized test) and chronological age; An IQ between 90 and 110 is considered average; over 120, superior; It is an index of measured intelligence expressed as the ratio of tested mental age to chronological age, multiplied by 100 (<u>Alfred Binet</u>, <u>*Intelligence Testing*</u> 1896; Binet-Simon tests, 1905 & 1908; <u>Lewis Terman</u>, *Stanford-Binet scale*,1916)

LEP/Limited English Proficiency – individuals whose primary/native language is not English

LEA/Local Educational Agency – a school district

Measurement – assigning numbers or ratings; "the assignment of numerals to objects or events according to some rule" (Stanley Smith Stevens (1946); the numerical of the magnitude of one quantity relative to another (Mitchell, 1997)

NO Child Left Behind Act (2002) – legislation passed by the U.S. Congress and signed into law by President Bush in 2002 as a federal education policy to improve America's public schools

Opportunity Gap - differences in resources available to different schools, such as: buildings, money and teachers, and other resources such as those in the community and at home: neighborhood libraries, personal computers and home reference materials

Professional Development – the ongoing training of teachers and school staff

Proficiency – a student being able to do something he or she is supposed to do at that age and grade level

"SOB" – Son of a bitch (a vulgar or offensive expression)

Summative Assessment – an assessment generally carried out at the end of a course or objective

Supplemental Services – services provided outside the regular school day to help students reach proficiency. These are paid for with federal Title I funds.

References and Selected Bibliographies

Armstrong, Thomas. (1994). *Multiple Intelligences in the Classroom.* Alexandria: VA, ASCD. Retrieved 12 April 06 from: http://www.thomasarmstrong.com/multiple.Intelligences.htm.

Bennett, W. J., U.S. Secretary of Education et al. (1986). *What Works: Research About Teaching and Learning.* Washington, DC: U.S. Department of Education.

Berkin, C., et al. (2003). *Virginia Social Studies.* Illinois: Scott Foresman.

Bloom, H. et al., Retrieved Feb 18, 2006 from: http://www.coun.unic.ca/learn/program/hndouts/bloom.html (date

Boutin, F. & Chinien, C. "Characteristics of effective classroom management." Retrieved 8 Feb 06 from http://home.cc.umanitoba.ca/~fboutin/frame.html

Closing the Achievement gap. NGA Center for Best Practices, Washington, D.C. Retrieved on 4/9/06) <http://www.subnet.nga.org/educlear/achievement/

"Critical Issue: Ensuring Equitable Use of Education Technology." (1996). Retrieved May 15, 2006 frohttp://www.ncrel.org/sdrs/areas/issues/methods/technlgy/te400.htm.

Elliot, Collin C. (1990). *Differential Ability Scales DAS).* Psychological Corporation. Retrieved April 24, 2006 from http://www.answers.com/topic/ differential-ability-scales?hl=achievement&hl=test

Ennis, R. (2006). *ABC Book.* Pennington School, Manassas, VA.

Fair Test: The National Center for Fair & Open Testing. Cambridge: MA. Retrieved April 26, 2006 from http://www.fairtest.org/facts/csrtests.html.

Ferguson, R. F. (1998). Can schools narrow the black-white test score gap? In C. Jencks and M. Phillips (Eds.), *the black-white test score gap* (pp. 318-374). Washington, DC: Brookings Institution.

Galbo, Cindy. (1998). "Helping Adults learn: New Research on Best Practice for Professional Development and How Adults Learn Has Important Implications for Administrators." *Thrust for Educational Leadership,* No. 669278. San Francisco, CA. May/June, 1998.

Gana, C. (2006). *My ABC Book.* Pennington School, Manassas, Virginia.

Georgia Department of Education – *Closing the student achievement gap.*
    Atlanta, GA: http://www.doe.k12.ga.us/index.asp

Guthrie, Fran, IST presenter. (2005). *"What Good readers Do: From A to Z"* a handout from
    "Train for Reading Endurance" workshop.
    California Reading Association/CRA), Costa Mesa, CA.

Gutloff, K., editor. (1996). *Integrated Thematic Teaching.*
    West Heaven, CT: NEA Professional Library.

Gutloff, K., editor. (1996). *Multiple Intelligences.* West Heaven,
    CT: NEA Professional Library.

Hargreaves, A., editor. (1997). *Rethinking Educational Change With Heart and Mind.*
    Alexandria, VA: ASCD.

Haycock, K. (2002). State policy levers: Closing the achievement gap. *The State Education
    Standard, 3,* 6-13. Education Trust (ET). Retrieved April 16, 2006 from
    http://www.ncrel.org/gap/library/text/schoolsmatter.htm

Henry, D. J. (2004). *The Effective Reader.* New York, NY: Pearson Longman.

Idio, I. (2004). *Effective School Leadership: A Handbook for Aspiring and Experienced Leaders.*
    Bloomington, Indiana: Authorhouse

Indiana Accountability System for Academic Progress Indiana Department of Education
    Contact: webmaster@doe.state.in.us

Kreml, N. M. et al. (2001). *College Writing: Reading, Analyzing and Writing.*
    New York, NY: Longman.

"Lovetoteach." (2006). Retrieved 2/2/06 from
    http://teachers.net/mentors/special_education/topic12883/1.29.06.07.54.html.

Lyle, A. (2006). *My End-of-The-Year ABC Book.* Pennington School Manassas, Virginia.

Manley, M. (2006). *Mike's ABC Book.* Pennington School Manassas, Virginia.

Marzano, Robert J. et al. (2001). *A Handbook for Classroom Instruction that Works.*
Alexandria: VA, ASCD.

McAlpine, J. et al. (1985). *What If?* San Luis Obispo, CA: Dandy Lion Publications.

Mitchell, J. (1997). "Quantitative science and the definition of measurement in psychology.
British Journal of Psychology, 88 355-383. Retrieved April 18, 2006
from http://www.answers.com

Mooney, M. E. (1990). *Reading to, With, and by Children.*
Katonah, NY: Richard C. Owen Publishers, Inc.

No Child Left Behind Act: A Quality Education for Every Child in America. (2002).
At: http://www.edmin.com/news/nclb/files/2_15.pdf

Other learning Styles links. Retrieved April 24, 2006 from
http://members.shaw.ca/priscillatheroux/styles.html.

Rheault., K. W., Superintendent of Public Instruction. *School Improvement Through Student
Achievement Gap Elimination.* NEVADA DOE.
Retrieved April 13, 06 from: http://www.nevadasage.org/home/contact.html

Rothman, R. (2001/02). *The Journal of the Annenburg Challenge. Vol 5, No. 2.*
Retrieved April 11, 2006 from: April 11, 06
http://www.annenberginstitute.org/challenge/pubs/cj/gap_cj.htm#approaches

Rutherford, P. (2002). *Why Didn't I Learn This in College.*
Alexandria: VA Just ASK Publications.

Sampson, Anthony. (1999). *Mandela: the Authorised Biography.*
Retrieved April 24, 2006 from: http://en.wikipedia.org/wiki/Nelson_Mandela.

Shay, J. Ph.D. (2004) "Understanding Comprehension Strategies" A handout at a workshop,
Pennington School, Manassas, VA.

Sledge, M., compiler. (2003). *The Longman Textbook Reader.* New York, NY: Addison
Wesley Longman, Inc.

Stevens, J., & Goldberg, D. (2001). *For the learners' sake: Brain-based instruction for the 21st century.*
Tucson, AR: Zephyr Press, p. 127.

Steven, S.S. (1946). *On the theory of scales of measurement.* Science, 103 667-80. Retrieved April 18, 2006 from http://www.answers.com.

Sugai, George. *Positive Behavior Intervention Support (PBIS).* A handout from Carolyn Lamm, ITS, at a workshop on "Challenging Behaviors/Classroom Management" PWCS, March 8 & 14, 2006.

Terman, L. (1916). "Stanford Revision of the Binet-Simon Scale." Retrieved April 252006 from http://www.answers.com/main/ntquery?method=4&tname=stanford-binet-iq-test&curtab=2050_1&linktext=Stanford-Binet%20scale.

Thinking Maps Inc., Cary: NC office@thinkingmaps.com Retrieved April 11, 200 From: http://www.nhcs.k12.nc.us/htree/Curriculum/ThinkingMaps.html#top

US Department of Education. (2005). "The 2005 Assessment Results" National Canter for Educational Statistics (NCES, 2005). Retrieved April 30, 2005 from http://nces.ed.gov/nationsreportcard/nrc/_reading_math_2005/s0003.asp?tab_id=tab2&subtab_id=Tab_1&printver=#chart

Vandermey, R., et al. (2004). *The College Writer.* NY, NY: Houghton Mifflin Company.

Weber, E. (1999). *Student assessment that works: A practical approach.* Allyn & Bacon, p. 31

Comment/Suggestion Form

Use this form to write your comments about this book and your suggestions for future editions.

_____

_____

_____

_____

_____

_____

_____

_____

_____

_____

_____

_____

_____

_____

_____

_____

Send your suggestions to:

5475 Middlebourne Lane
Centreville, VA 20120
E-mail: iidio@aol.com

Or

AuthorHouse
1663 Liberty Drive, Suite 200
Bloomington, Indiana 47403
www.authorhouse.com

INDEX

ABOUT THE AUTHOR

Dr. Ignatius E. Idio is the author of *Effective School Leadership: A Handbook for Aspiring and Experienced Leaders*, as well as, the award winning poetries of inspiration and courage entitled: "Bravo to NASA," published in *Many Voices Many Lands by Anthology of Poetry, vl No. 1, 1987* and "Before My Journey Ends," published in *Expressions by American Poets Society, 2005*.

Dr. Idio earned his Ph.D. in educational leadership and administration from Argosy University of Sarasota, Sarasota, Florida; an M.S. in elementary education from Gramblng State University, Grambling, Louisiana; and a B.A. in economics from Fort Valley State University, Fort Valley, Georgia.

He is also an adjunct professor of English at Northern Virginia Community College Manassas Campus and a seasoned public school educator and teacher with Prince William County Public Schools district in Manassas, Virginia.

Dr. Idio is an active member of the Association for Supervision and Curriculum Development (ASCD), the National Education Association (NEA), and the Uruan Development Association (UDA) USA, Inc (a nonprofit, charitable organization) where he serves as the current general secretary and chair of the UDA scholarship committee. He has done extensive consultation work for school administrators and teachers. In 2005, he served on the Akwa Ibom Association of Nigeria USA, Inc. subcommittee on Academic Excellence Project and coauthored the "Criteria for Academic Excellence." He was twice elected to *Who's Who Among Students in American Universities & Colleges*.

Dr. Idio brings to the book his extensive and practical experience teaching in the public schools and higher education, as well as, acquired research-based best teaching practices and strategies that teachers and instructors can use to teach all students in order to eradicate achievement gap between minority, disadvantage students and their more affluent majority counterparts.

He may be contacted at 5475 Middlebourne Lane, Centreville, VA 20120.
Phone: (703)-968-7984/362-9172. E-mail: iidio@aol.com.

Printed in the United States
75333LV00007B/48